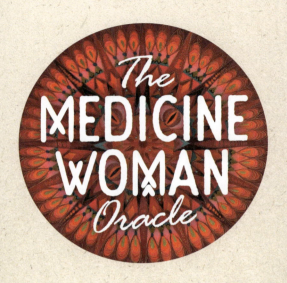

The MEDICINE WOMAN Oracle

CATHERINE MAILLARD
Illustrated by Caroline Manière

A Rockpool book
PO Box 252
Summer Hill
NSW 2130
Australia

rockpoolpublishing.com

Follow us! **f** ⓞ rockpoolpublishing
Tag your images with #rockpoolpublishing

First published in France in 2020 as L'oracle des femmes
médecine, ISBN 9782702917824 by Le Courrier du Livre.

This edition published in 2022 by Rockpool Publishing

ISBN: 9781922579409

Design by Sara Lindberg, Rockpool Publishing
Edited by Jess Cox

Printed and bound in China
10 9 8 7 6 5 4 3 2

PREFACE

I have chosen to be a woman, artist and keeper of medicine women. These women come to me, to you. They pass on their messages; share their experience, wisdom and power; offer their brightness, vibration and powerful energy; and accompany us with their medicine. They come to reveal and awaken what is buried within us. They remind us of our connection to the Great All and to our Mother Earth. They enable us to deeply experience the polarity, the essence, that we have come here as women to embody.

Each painting channels and diffuses a powerful message of love, destined to accompany, challenge, deploy and comfort you and to help you heal ...

Through these images, symbols, patterns and words, I pay homage to the woman we all are – powerful, connected, vulnerable and dreamy; a healer, warrior, magician, mother and daughter ... These women are all One.

I discovered these many facets on a long journey of inner psychological and spiritual work. They reflect that part of ourselves we can barely recognise – that beauty, purity, sacredness and wisdom we often forget to reconnect to, tend and honour.

May these powerful archetypes remind you of who you are – your value, richness and gifts – and enable you to celebrate your femininity and connection to the Great All, in their vastness and sacredness.

Caroline Manière

CONTENTS

GIFTS OF THE FEMININE CARDS 63

TOTEMS/ALLIED SPIRITS CARDS 101

MEDICINE ACTION CARDS 139

ACKNOWLEDGEMENTS 177

BIBLIOGRAPHY 179

ABOUT THE AUTHOR 181

ABOUT THE ARTIST 183

INTRODUCTION

MOTHER EARTH CALLS US ...

Every day I commit to the world, as a woman, citizen, she-wolf, elder and author. I dream to see the world aligned with life, our deep essence and nature, and with our own nature ... I have faith in the feminisation of the world, with greater roundness, gentleness, emotion, intuition, mystery, poetry and peace, where we once again honour our ancestors, Mother Earth and ancient wisdom.

... CAN YOU HEAR HER SONG?

The Medicine Woman Oracle is your guide on this journey of awakening the feminine, and of healing your wounds.

The oracle was born from the medicine wheel of deep femininity, the teaching of the Keepers of the 13 Moons, and the guidance offered by my totems, Mother Bear and Snowy Owl, who breathe messages of wisdom and sisterhood into my life. In women's circles, we share secrets, as well as laughter and support, tears and treason and rituals. Together – teachers, friends, mothers, grandmothers, young girls – we are all united, in our hearts, souls, bellies and moccasins. I wish you a fabulous encounter with yourself in the magic of the feminine, celebrating the return of the Great Goddess.

AWAKENING THE FEMININE

Women are on the move, towards themselves, towards their essence!

In these times of great change, women are gathering with the intention of reconnecting to their true essence, reawakening their life force ... and changing the world. A new women's revolution is on the horizon, inspired by ancient wisdom and aligned with values connected to women's true nature, and of awakening to a new awareness. More and more women are joining circles dedicated to them, on issues such as maternity, ancestral wisdom, sexuality, the seasons or the moon. These women share a common journey: from healing wounds to awakening the sacred feminine.

The Medicine Woman Oracle **invites you to embark on this journey with us.**

The roots of this movement are found in the need to reconnect to our feminine aspect, which has been left fallow. Women occupy greater space today than before. To make a place for ourselves, however, we have forced our beings into predominantly masculine models. How could it have been any other way? In our society, where the prevailing need is to domesticate nature and develop technology that controls the world, we have had no choice but to try to become equal to men ... by becoming like them. Genders have become confused, which is not without risk. By enclosing ourselves in armour to be efficient, we have forgotten to be vessels. By holding fast to defensive or aggressive positions, we have cut away our feelings and vital strengths. It is difficult to reconcile feminine values (being receptive, open and embracing) with our hard-won social roles! But it is that inner journey, of reconnecting to feminine values, that we must accomplish.

We must also free ourselves from an ancient story. Something that resonated with me is what Aude de Thuin, founder of the Women's Forum, said at a meeting: 'In this patriarchal system, women's relationship to men as protectors has always been the foundation of their existence, which is why women are in a permanent state of insecurity from having to depend on a physically and socially more powerful being ... in order to survive.' This insecurity has left traces in our own stories. Among the challenges we women face is the need to free ourselves from old patterns and participate fully in the world, which requires us to regain confidence in our values.

This work of empowerment is what we have to accomplish.

NEW KEYS ON THE PATH

1. ANCESTRAL WISDOM AND RITUAL ARTS

One of the International Council of Thirteen Indigenous Grandmothers, Wilma Mankiller, once said, 'Among elders, it is said that women will be the ones to carry the awakening of awareness, and that they are called to gather.' Women's bodies are subject to the great cycles of the moon and stars, and women's wisdom is connected to the earth and sky. Created in 2004, the council includes wise women, *curanderas*, shamans and healers from the four corners of the globe. They emphasise maintaining the sacred ties between people and the land, and present a path of wisdom in which rituals, prayer and plant-based medicine are paramount. Inspired by this ancestral wisdom, many women's circles are being created worldwide; these help each woman to realise her gifts and personal talents to restore this lost harmony.

2. SEARCHING FOR SISTERHOOD

Women's circles are also called the 'cauldron' or 'matrix' by the crones. In times past, women gathered and shared their wisdom, living and acting within women's circles. On the occasion of their first 'moon time' (their period), young women were initiated and welcomed into the 'women's line'. They had become ready to receive the 'moon wisdom' from those who had walked before them. This ancestral tradition has passed the tests of time – as evidenced by the emergence of red tents (taken from the title of Anita Diamant's landmark novel). Today, red tents are gatherings of women in intimate settings dedicated to them that aim to hand down wisdom through sharing women's stories, secrets and questions on the nature of the feminine. There, women can find a community of people who share feminine values and support each other. And in these circles, the seeds of sisterhood – in which each woman can once again honour her roots, cycles and ties to nature and the unseen – can flourish.

3. RETURN TO OUR BODIES

In our feminine awakening, the body, our temple, is of central importance. Reappropriating our bodies is our foremost, even if unconscious, need. After a long period of disenchantment, the body is now returning to grace. For too long, we have been busy hunting wrinkles and cellulite, ignorant of the magic of our cycles and natural beauty. Today, our challenge is to not hurry over reconnecting to our deep, wild and free natures. Our beautiful energy sometimes struggles to find its path due to the 'organic' and 'psychological' waste (undigested emotions, pains and shocks) that has been stored. But there are many ways we can reconnect to our physiological rhythms and our eternal ally – our body – such as summoning our 'wild' body memories, shamanic practices, dancing and body psychotherapy. When our energy is released, we find ourselves with renewed vitality and we discover our creative power. That is our treasure!

4. THE SACRED FEMININE

In the West, the sacred feminine is being renewed: the 'call of the Goddess'. Women secretly aspire to return to mystery and mystique; we have both the ability and taste for transcendence. We need rituals and ceremonies such as sacred dances, chants and teachings. We celebrate the life force that unites us all, the matrix waters of our beginnings, the primordial memory we carry, the beauty and power of women. We aspire to reawaken women's memories from time immemorial, when we venerated the creative divinity, the Great Goddess, who gives life, nourishes, heals, transforms and watches over her children. A time when we were priestesses dedicated to the worship of Goddess and Mother Earth.

PRESENTING THE ORACLE

'[V]iolence against the native peoples, the land, and
so much of Nature destroyed the Earth's balance and
dissipated the feminine energy of the planet ... Women must
wake up this great force they possess and bring the world
back to peace and harmony.'

Carol Schaefer

Together, we have a wonderful opportunity in this feminine
awakening of awareness. We have incredible resources at
our disposal to weave the pattern of a dream for the world
of tomorrow. We need to reawaken our ancestral memories,
connect to the energy of the divine feminine archetypes,
summon our allies of shamanic wisdom and practise rituals
to transform our wounds. To regain confidence in our gifts
we must let the infinite mystery of life flow through us,
inspire us and plant its seeds in us.

A woman is a fabulous, multifaceted collection of
enchantments. The magic of menstrual cycles, echoing the
course of Lady Moon, is planted in our bodies. The seeds
of the Great Sacred Dream are sown in the temple of our
belly, our uterus – the primordial matrix of life, according to
the old crones. Our sexuality, cradle of the kundalini snake,
energy of the deeps, rekindles the fire of Shiva's great
cosmic dance, Shakti.

In *The Medicine Woman Oracle*, we will call upon various forms of wisdom to reconnect with the true nature of the feminine.

SHAMANIC WISDOM

Shamanism carries a spiritual ancestral heritage. This wisdom has been rediscovered mainly through the writings of ethnologist Mircea Eliade: 'Within it, we are all considered "cosmic voyagers" living our journey on Earth based on the model of the cycles of the sun and moon, the four seasons, and the cardinal points.' We are not separate from nature, but a part of it. This wisdom offers a philosophy and practices to exist in harmony with all realms living on our beautiful planet, and to celebrate the sacredness of our lives. More recently, in her book *The 13 Original Clan Mothers*, Jamie Sams shares a medicine wheel aimed at healing the deep feminine. The medicine wheel proposes a shamanic framework dedicated to the feminine.

RITUAL PRACTICES

Ancestral traditions remind us of the importance of ceremonies to maintain the sacred ties between people and the earth. Sacredness is a primary aspect of the ritual arts and is common to all practices, beyond time and traditions. Ethnologist Mircea Eliade defined 'sacredness' as 'something contrary to the secular world, a breach through which the extraordinary dimension of life can manifest'. In times past, ritualised activities of breaking with the day to day had a sacred quality that allowed visions and magic to appear.

The Medicine Woman Oracle offers ritualised practices to open this sacred space and receive inspiring messages and healing on your journey.

THE WILD FEMININE

According to Jungian analyst Clarissa Pinkola Estés, who shaped the concept in 1992, the wild feminine is the primordial resource of the feminine essence: 'A healthy woman is much like a wolf: robust, chock-full, strong life force, life-giving, territorially aware, inventive, loyal, roving.'

To evoke a woman's wild nature is to refer to her instinctive force that manifests spontaneously in the service of life. Where is the wild feminine today? How can we restore its rightful place in our modern times?

The wild feminine is present in *The Medicine Woman Oracle*. It whispers throughout the pages of this guidebook, runs with you through the trees and reveals your original nature.

THE RETURN OF ARCHETYPES

The Great Goddess has returned, as many feminist uprisings throughout the world can attest: 'After 2,000 years of repressing the life instinct, the soul, and the wisdom of the Great Goddess, Isis, powerful solar goddess of Ancient Egypt, breathes her mythical energy once more to invigorate our times with feminine values,' explains psychoanalyst Marie-Laure Colonna. In the Goddess's wake, feminine archetypes are emerging – Demeter, Artemis, the Dakini, the Loba, Ostara, Kali – as are witches, rehabilitating Hecate (the secretly venerated Olympian goddess with multiple powers), Circe, Mélusine and her sisters and, with them, medicine women, healers and herbalists.

In *The Medicine Woman Oracle* we will journey with these 13 aspects of women found in ancestral wisdom and myths, symbolising women's untameable strength, ecofeminist and shamanic values – to restore awareness of the Great Goddess and awaken to the wisdom of Mother Earth.

THE CARDS' MEDICINE PATH

It is time to honour the gift we received at birth: of being a woman, an incredible gift of life. We will venture on a path of initiation and explore our feminine essence to recover our vital strengths. We will rise to stand tall again, and manifest the great dream of Pachamama for her children.

The Medicine Woman Oracle opens the way and offers the keys for us to reconnect to women's ancestral wisdom, healing wounds and awakening the feminine.

STRUCTURE OF THIS ORACLE

In the shamanic tradition, all is circle, or cycle. Our journey towards healing and feminine empowerment will travel different circles.

The 49 cards in *The Medicine Woman Oracle* are divided into four circles:

1. 13 archetypal medicine woman cards
2. 12 gifts of the feminine cards
3. 12 shamanic allied spirits (or totems) cards
4. 12 medicine action cards

Each card includes a message that offers symbolic keys at the level of the psyche; words of guidance for interpretation and practical indications for your life; and a practice to awaken the card with a resource: a healing medicine, prayer or ritual for transformation and change.

THE 13 MEDICINE WOMEN

Each medicine woman relates to a teaching found in ancestral shamanic wisdom and carries a medicine, or totem. The presence of a medicine woman in a spread will guide you to restore your awareness of the Great Goddess, and awaken you to the wisdom of Mother Earth.

THE FEMININE GIFTS

The Medicine Woman Oracle proposes a maiden quest to discover the inherent gifts of the feminine. These are the 12 talents of our feminine essence, our *anima*. In ancestral traditions, woman is the keeper of universal sacred laws, ensuring all forms of life have their rightful place in the great sacred circle. They are the yin aspect of the wheel, an inner journey.

THE TOTEMS/ALLIED SPIRITS

In shamanic traditions the medicine wheel represents the universe, or the 'Great All', which contains all things. The medicine wheel is divided into four cardinal points – north, south, east and west. Each cardinal point is usually associated with a season, animal and element (earth, water, fire and air). By calling upon these allied spirits we can connect to earth's primordial forces and restore lost harmony. Each allied spirit carries a specificity, which the shamans call 'medicine power' – a force they will pass on to you.

MEDICINE ACTION

To rehabilitate our original nature, we need to find our medicine: to heal our ancient memories, kindle the flame of life and invite its growth, and stand tall on the path of our rebirth. Then, we will discover an unvanquished strength deep within us, a natural authority and unbelievable strength. This active practice proposes healing the wounds of the past to re-enchant the world with our divine presence, our chants and our drums. It is the yang aspect of the wheel, a journey of empowerment.

THE ART OF DIVINATION

Oracles are messages delivered by a divinity through an intermediary – a man or woman dedicated to this art. In ancient times, the term 'oracle' (*oracula*) referred to the answers given by the gods to humans who came to consult them, as well as to the places where those answers were sought. Through *The Medicine Woman Oracle*, you will reconnect with an ancestral tradition of divination. You can receive messages in many ways: through a card reading, the murmur of a stream, the song of the wind through a tree, or the tale told by an old crone. Fate often brings insights into the Oracle's answers and, in such cases, happy coincidences happen in echo, signs of the profound wisdom contained in the art of divination.

HOW TO USE THE CARDS

Your copy of *The Medicine Woman Oracle* is a personal possession, a ritual object. As soon as you receive it you can assume an alliance with your oracle to grant it the power to connect you to the unseen worlds, the great mystery, the divine. In this way you will awaken your gift of divination, the thousand eyes of your intuition and your psychic channel. Store your oracle in a place dedicated to that purpose, where the energy is especially positive.

CREATING SPREADS

In ancient times oracles were consulted in temples, allowing the divinity to express their message. When you wish to do a reading, re-create that sacred space to invite the spirit of the medicine woman within it and receive her oracle.

THE SACRED SPACE

Select a piece of fabric symbolising divination to you, on which to spread your cards. While purple is traditionally associated with spiritual dimensions, feel free to make your own choices. Place your representation of the Great Goddess (such as an image or small statue) before you, and a candle. If you have one, bring your drum or rattle.

THE INTENTION

Voice your question clearly so your request may be heard. Aim to choose an open-ended question, such as 'How may I create the most favourable conditions to … [find love, support my project, my health, etc.]?' Or 'Which wisdom/medicine/talent do I need in this situation?'

THE SPREAD, STEP BY STEP

Light your candle, then draw an imaginary circle around you to open a reading ritual with the oracle. Prepare to enter the sacred land, where the voices of divinity, myths and legends, the Great Sacred Dream and Mother Earth all resound.

Take *The Medicine Woman Oracle* card deck in your hands and hold it to your heart. Invoke the cards' support, and thank them for the help they will give you. Shuffle the cards with confidence and awareness of the dance of all potentialities in your hands.

With your left hand – your intuitive hand – fan out the cards before you. Ask your question out loud, giving the energy of your request density in the physical world. Close your eyes. Let your fingers run over the cards laid out before you. A card will call to you.

Place your selected card before you face down, and engage in divinatory dialogue. Turn the card over and embrace its message. Look at the imagery; let it speak to your unconscious. Write down everything that comes to mind – your physical sensations, your emotions – everything has significance. Read the card's sentence and let it resonate like a mantra throughout your day.

Turn to the guidebook to discover the answer the oracle has given you. The oracle consciously invites you to journey on the medicine wheel of awakening the feminine. The card's message provides you with symbolic keys. Let yourself be inspired by this teaching.

Let the connections establish themselves naturally between the seen and unseen worlds. This practice invites you to awaken the card with a resource, healing medicine, prayer, or ritual for transformation and change.

Take up your drum or rattle to establish a direct link with the Medicine Woman, or your allied spirits or totems. You can also play sacred or shamanic music. This step is a phase of integration, ritualisation and alliance with the oracle, which will bring the power of the feminine into your life.

GIVING THANKS

To close the ritual, gather up the cards and return them to their box. Fold your piece of fabric and, if you like, wrap it around your box of cards. Take a moment to give thanks for all you have received and for the medicine woman. Blow out your candle.

In the days that follow, keep an eye out for synchronicities, unusual perceptions or changes. You can write them down in a notebook dedicated to your quest of awakening the feminine to celebrate each new step forward on the path and foster your trust in the process.

THE ORACLE SPREADS

You can obtain answers and support from *The Medicine Woman Oracle* in various ways. Each spread enables you to forge ties with the medicine women, ensuring they will protect and guide you on your path of evolution.

DAILY WISDOM

This practice involves drawing a single card from the deck to request a message for your day ahead. While remaining focused on your intention, shuffle the cards. Fan them out before you and quickly choose a card. Let yourself be inspired by the imagery and sentence; these will be your mantra for the day. Put the card somewhere in plain sight. Before going to bed, thank the medicine women and return the card to the deck.

CALL THE MEDICINE WOMEN

To establish dialogue with the medicine women you do a single-card reading (see above) to obtain insight into a specific question and discover your medicine or great power. Consult the medicine women regularly. With practise, you will feel their presence and receive their precious legacy of wisdom. Over time you will become a medicine woman yourself in your own life.

THE MEDICINE WHEEL

This is a full spread with four steps. Set aside an hour dedicated to this spread if you can. Divide the deck into four categories, and set them down before you in four piles:

1. The circle of the 13 medicine women
   (removing the 13th card)
2. The circle of the gifts of the feminine
3. The circle of the totems/allied spirits
4. The circle of medicine action

Take time to prepare yourself for your medicine wheel ritual (see pages 16–18). Set your intention: to explore your next stage on the medicine wheel of awakening the feminine.

Step 1. Fan out the first pile. Ask your question: 'Which medicine woman shares her teaching?' Let yourself be called by a card, then set it aside face down.

Step 2. Fan out the second pile. Ask your question: 'What innate talent do I have to travel gracefully on the feminine medicine wheel?' Let yourself be called by a card, then set it to the right of the first card face down.

Step 3. Fan out the third pile. Ask your question: 'Which totem/allied spirit guides me gracefully on the feminine medicine wheel?' Let yourself be called by a card, then set it below the second card face down.

Step 4. Fan out the fourth pile. Ask your question: 'Which medicine action must I carry out to awaken the feminine medicine wheel?' Let yourself be called by a card, then set it below the first card face down.

Taking your time, turn each card over one at a time. Visually embrace the woman you are at this moment – it is an important medicine consultation. Then, at your own pace, turn to the guidebook for information about each of the four aspects of your wheel. To awaken the medicine wheel, carry out one of the rituals/practices suggested on your cards. Give thanks. Your journey with *The Medicine Woman Oracle* opens the way towards an important transformation under the medicine women's loving and benevolent protection.

In the days that follow, keep an eye out for the effects of this experience.

ARCHETYPAL
MEDICINE
WOMEN CARDS

Each medicine woman relates to a teaching found in
ancestral shamanic wisdom and carries a medicine,
a totem, symbolising women's untameable strength
and her ecofeminist and divine values. The presence
of a medicine woman in a spread will guide you on the
path to restoring awareness of the Great Goddess and
awaken you to the wisdom of Mother Earth.

I. INTERCONNECTION

I BRING YOU THE MEDICINE OF TOGETHERNESS.

⫸ MESSAGE ⫷

I am a keeper of the interconnection between different realms. I know the magic that connects us all – plants, minerals, animals and humans. Each takes their place in the great circle of life, and great harmony depends on our awareness of this link. Spirits are everywhere, and we – the seen and unseen – have the ability to converse together. All is the wheel. We all carry a part of the Great Sacred Dream; we are all connected. I come to you to revive your deep affinity for friendliness, sharing and encounters; true jubilation is to be found in togetherness.

'It is by becoming aware of our interconnection with Nature and other species that we will be able to face environmental challenges and build a viable future.'

Satish Kumar

⫷⫷ GUIDANCE ⫸⫸

The time has come to move from 'I' to 'we'. The Medicine Woman of Interconnection invites you to be more aware of our interconnections with nature: plants, minerals and animals. Feel, communicate and ritualise. With humans too. Develop knowledge to reinvent your collective ties and make them more cooperative and communal. You may have experienced disappointments in your relationships; move beyond this pitfall. Find your allies. They are all around you, making the world a better place for you and other species, together.

⫷⫷ AWAKEN YOUR MEDICINE ⫸⫸

Connect to this archetype and set the foundations for deep ecology by re-establishing an exceptional dialogue with the world around you.

Open your ritual space. Ask yourself: how do I create relationships with life, with nature? Choose one of your own plants, or a tree in the forest, or your cat. Take a moment to be silent and listen. Become aware that you share the same air, the same sun, the same water. What can you do for them? Water them, hug them, play with them. Observe what this awareness changes in your own behaviour. Then, do the same thing with a person close to you; take this time with no other motive than the encounter.

'By developing a considerate relationship with your immediate environment, you are the new weaver of the world, of ties between species – a key to the conservation of biodiversity.'

II. GREAT MYSTERY

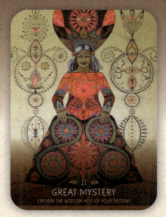

I REVEAL THE WISDOM KEYS
OF YOUR DESTINY.

⫷ MESSAGE ⫸

I am the crone, the grandmother. I watch over you
constantly. I frequent the great mystery, which hands you
the keys to the secrets of your destiny. My connection to
the science of the stars and dance of the planets gives me

great wisdom – trust in my messages. My spirit is full of old memories, and I talk to the ancestors. I am the ancestral knowledge contained within the cycle of time and sacred legends. I guide you with love on your life's path, and I light the way to your destiny. You can call on me to better understand your life experiences and embrace them. Through me, your ancestors send you their messages and protection.

'Life will give you whatever experience is most helpful for the evolution of your consciousness.'

Eckhart Tolle

⫷⫷ GUIDANCE ⫸⫸

The time has come to lift a corner of the great mystery's veil and orient yourself on your life's path. The Medicine Woman of Great Mystery benevolently encourages you to discover who you truly are, and what your next step will be. She brings you greater confidence in your evolutionary processes. Explore the mystery of your roots; have your astrological or numerological birth chart done; make an appointment with your therapist ... Something is in the works, and you are blessed and protected. This is your time; take stock on what you have learned and draw life lessons from your experiences. Your wisdom is growing.

⫷⫷ AWAKEN YOUR MEDICINE ⫸⫸

Connect with this archetype to identify the gift or life lesson in the experience you are going through: a signpost on your path, your destiny.

Open your ritual space. Take up your drum, burn some sage to embrace your ancestors' memories and ask your question. What memory watches over you? What wisdom, what life lesson, is the memory passing down to you? Explore! Let the images and messages come to you. Ask to receive the wisdom of your ancestors, now and for future generations. Give thanks. Then, be open to synchronicities and meaningful encounters throughout the day. Trust that you have been heard, and your prayer has been answered.

'Celebrate each step; only you can know, in the deep wisdom of your heart, what has brought you to this point!'

III. AUTHENTICITY

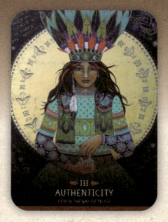

III
AUTHENTICITY
I OPEN THE WAY OF TRUTH

I OPEN THE WAY OF TRUTH.

⫷ MESSAGE ⫸

I am the light of truth, and I benevolently encourage your quest for authenticity. I know the power of integrity that frees the shoulders from the burdens we carry, of cultural conditioning and transgenerational legacies. I bring my protection to those who wonder why things are what they are and what the fundamental truth of life is. I am the greatness of the clarity of the sacred laws before you, and the courage to honour them. Be assured of my presence when you feel confusion, and of my protection when you experience deceit or manipulation. With me at your side the truth will always be revealed in the end.

≪≪ GUIDANCE ≫≫

This card supports you in your search for authenticity. 'Be true,' whispers the medicine woman. 'You are under my protection.' What truth does your heart hold? Have the courage to raise the banner of who you truly are. Remember, too, there is no single truth; embrace the truth of another. This oracle gives you the ability to detect lies – a quality innate from childhood. Be attentive to signs; they provide information about the person or situation that concerns you. In this way you can detect any lack of integrity. Sometimes, for different reasons, we lie to ourselves; it is time to honour your truth and release limiting illusions to let the purity of your heart finally resound.

≪≪ AWAKEN YOUR MEDICINE ≫≫

Invoke the Medicine Woman of Authenticity to shed light on your truth, or a situation or person.

Open your ritual space. Light a candle, a symbol of light. Acquire a crystal, a symbol of purity. Cover your head with a veil or your face with a theatre mask (plain or decorated), representing the lack of clarity in lies. Ask your question. Bring the light of truth to the situation or person that concerns you. What do you feel? What do you see? Who is hiding behind the mask? Explore! Visualise the situation or person in a bubble illuminated by crystalline light. Then, remove the veil or mask and ask the medicine for its support in expressing your truth out loud. Write down your truth, dance it, draw it.

'Commit to sharing it with benevolence to move forward on your path. Feel the lightness after having removed the veils of illusion.'

IV. VISION

◈ IV ◈
VISION
I GIVE YOU CONFIDENCE IN YOUR DIVINATION TALENTS.

I GIVE YOU CONFIDENCE IN YOUR DIVINATION TALENTS.

⟪⟪⟪ MESSAGE ⟫⟫⟫

I am the oracle, the medium, the one who sees beyond
the veil of appearances. My eye is piercing; it knows the
depths of your soul and the bravery in your heart. My gift
is also yours: I receive messages from the universe, from

the Great Spirit, so all may find their place in keeping the sacred order. Divination is an ancestral art held by the prophetesses; it is a great feminine power. My sisters read the signs in ground coffee, the song of the wind or the art of runes. I am here to release your magical talents and re-enchant the world.

⋘ GUIDANCE ⋙

The time has come to awaken your inner vision. The universe is speaking to you! The medicine woman tenderly opens your vision channel to weave the connection of magical alliance and co-create a world of harmony. You already have a deep interest in astrology, tarots, dream symbolism or ritualised practices. To interpret events and orient your life, harness your visionary talents and explore your divination supports. Go through the looking glass to discover other worlds. A divine opportunity is presenting itself: you are benefiting from a peak of intuition, so ask questions; request help in bringing a meaningful project to fruition. This card indicates that this is a good time to carry out a particular ancestral shamanic ritual: the vision quest.

≪≪≪ AWAKEN YOUR MEDICINE ≫≫≫

Connect to this archetype, and ask to receive a vision for your life through your dreams.

Open your ritual space. When you go to bed, set your intention. In the world between reality and dreams, it is possible to receive messages or presages from ancestors or another form of reality. If you have a dreamcatcher, hang it above your bed as a signal. Invoke the Medicine Woman of Vision, and ask her to encourage spirits to visit, bearing messages for dreamers. Give thanks, and let yourself wander into the realm of dreams.

When you wake up, take notes and plan for a time that day to create a vision board. Using a piece of paper with cut-outs from magazines, drawings, written notes and any other materials you like, manifest your vision.

'Trust that you have been heard, and your prayer answered.'

V. DEEP LISTENING

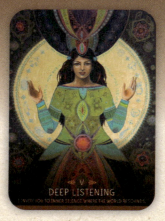

DEEP LISTENING

I INVITE YOU TO INNER SILENCE, WHERE THE WORLD RESOUNDS.

I INVITE YOU TO INNER SILENCE,
WHERE THE WORLD RESOUNDS.

⋘ MESSAGE ⋙

I am Listening, the keeper of inner silence. I offer you this space to embrace the murmur of the world and the heart of all life. Open up your inner ear to discover my presence there, and silence your ever-chattering mind.

New languages now appear: the voices of birds, the melody of rivers, the wind blowing through trees. Spirits' messages can now come to you. So often we ask questions without listening to the answers. Deep listening is my medicine on your path of awakening the feminine. It opens the realm of feeling, letting you access precious experiences of sharing in relationships and with nature. With me at your side, your being enters into resonance with the world.

'Elders used to tell us to just listen and the answers would come.'

Rita Pitka Blumenstein

⫷ GUIDANCE ⫸

The time has come to develop a new quality of presence in your relationships or with the world. Be assured the medicine woman grants you the magic of deep listening, the doorway to knowing someone. Honour this gift: listen to your loved ones without seeking to interrupt them or be right. Wonderment, joy and communion can then bloom from the encounter! Whether on a walk or before a beautiful landscape, some silences become deep, in which looks, small gestures and smiles prevail over speaking. In this 'living' silence, only the essential is expressed.

⋘ AWAKEN YOUR MEDICINE ⋙

Connect to this archetype, and take a moment to allow ritualised silence to open up your inner listening.

Open your ritual space. Sit in a calm place and come into contact with your own presence, as if you were diving deep into yourself. This is a time for contemplation. Close your eyes. Listen to your breathing and the perceptible beating of your heart. Honour this reconnection to yourself! Savour the feeling of fullness. In nature, take a silent walk with a loved one and listen to the songs of Mother Earth, the whispers of the wind, the song of a stream. Then awaken this space to hear them beyond words, without rushing to speak. Embrace the experience. Observe what changes in your relationship with that person.

'Trust in your medicine and in the process of transformation in your relationship to the world.'

VI. STORIES

VI
STORIES
I LEAVE YOU THE MEMORY OF HEALING TALES

I LEAVE YOU THE MEMORY OF HEALING TALES.

⋘ MESSAGE ⋙

I am the storyteller, the *curandera*. I am with you on your journey, every step of the way. I know the power of stories, tales and myths; they sharpen our view by helping us to follow the path set out by our psyche. My bag contains every enchantment and fairy tale, as well as fabulous allies from nature. I am she who teaches you to honour the oral traditions, the keepers of universal wisdom, which we all carry deep within us, bringing us back to our roots. Once upon a time, she was; today, she is; one day, she will be ... You can use the medicine of stories to banish your fears, dive deep into the flow of life and shed light on your personal legend. My stories are healing.

≪≪ GUIDANCE ≫≫

Your family history plays itself out, again and again, in the course of your life's flowing waters. This card indicates the time has come to own your family history, to understand its dynamics. The medicine woman gives you the opportunity to release the past and write your own story! Take your destiny into your hands; become the heroine of your own life. What role do you now play? Who do you want to be? Probe your family and loved ones for information. Hear the old stories, then re-create your own. Dive into tales, myths and legends, renewing resonances to re-enchant your life. Explore the art of tales; tell, play or write stories ... 'Your talent,' whispers the medicine woman.

⫷⫷ AWAKEN YOUR MEDICINE ⫸⫸

Connect to this archetype, and shed light on an episode in your life, creating a new reality in which past, present and future mingle for shining tomorrows.

Open your ritual space. Take up your drum, burn some sage and call the magic of stories. Let a situation come to you. Feel with all your senses: smells and sounds and tastes … What emotions do you feel? Why is this moment important? Dive deep and immerse yourself, like being in a story. You are the heroine; what is happening to you? Let connections to your lineage come to you; images and insights will appear. Does a particular tale inspire you? Write it down. Practise the art of storytelling by writing down your own life. Spend time on it. Then, share your own story! In ancestral traditions, sharing one's story was vital to integrating one's experience. What remains in awareness depends on how you will tell your story and share it.

You can also open a space for sharing tales with your family or friends. Ask: 'What did you experience yesterday or before that is significant to you and that you would like to share with us?'

'Our respective stories take on the aura of tales and offer a new outlook on our destiny.'

VII. UNCONDITIONAL LOVE

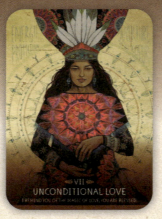

≪ VII ≫
UNCONDITIONAL LOVE
I REMIND YOU OF THE MAGIC OF LOVE. YOU ARE BLESSED.

I REMIND YOU OF THE MAGIC OF LOVE; YOU ARE BLESSED.

≪≪ MESSAGE ≫≫

I am the nurturing mother, she who takes care of all life on earth. I carry the medicine of unconditional love. I watch over you and all my children. By providing you with the memory of abundance, I ensure you'll want for nothing.

Invoke me to guide your steps onto fertile land, where you are safe to grow and develop your talents. My hand takes yours, giving you new courage. You are never alone. Love is my religion, my act of faith, my prayer that you will manifest kindness around you and develop a positive state of mind. Be assured: you are loved for all eternity. Through me, you can shine this love.

≪≪ GUIDANCE ≫≫

The time has come to take care of yourself, others and humanity. The medicine woman invites you, without delay, to let yourself act from the energy of the heart, of love, and be vulnerable. Pay attention to others; let yourself be moved. Does someone close to you need your help? She asks you to kindle the hearth fire's gentle flame. Whether you are alone or with your family, gather your tribe. Plan to spend time together with gratitude in your hearts. Take care of yourself too; how can you give yourself love? Be generous; life is showering you with blessings and abundance.

≪≪ AWAKEN YOUR MEDICINE ≫≫

Connect to this archetype, and illuminate your relationship to the mother, allowing deep, pure love to flow freely whatever your story!

Open your ritual space. Take up your drum, light a candle and acquire a piece of pink quartz – the crystal of the heart. Gather some pictures of your mother and the Divine Mother (Amma, the Virgin Mary, or others). Establish a heart connection to your mother, and let the love energy flow. If grievances and resentments arise, write them down on a piece of paper then burn the paper. Let messages of love for your mother, of gratitude for the gift of life, come to you. Write them down. Give thanks to all the mothers. Blow out your candle. Then, make the decision to become a good mother to yourself. What can you do to take care of yourself today? Treat yourself to the scent of lavender essential oil, for its maternal qualities.

'Let your heart speak! It is the best guide of all.'

VIII. HEALING

I SUPPORT YOU ON THE PATH OF HEALING.

⋘ MESSAGE ⋙

I am the healer, she who protects midwives, wise women and herbalists. I have inherited the magical knowledge of the cycles of life, death and rebirth. Call me for a smooth birthing or to help someone cross the threshold towards death. My deepest wish is to give all my support. My medicine heals the wounds of the soul and banishes negative energies from the body. The art of potions, philtres, elixirs and medicinal plants holds no secrets for me. I dry, I cut, I grind, I sing ... Trust in me, I am a powerful medicine woman, a witch.

⋘ GUIDANCE ⋙

The time for healing has come! In the cycle of transformation, you are about to cross the threshold: what must you let die? From which tragedy must you free yourself? We come to this earth with a transgenerational heritage that we are here to transmute. It is time to heal the wound of your soul to find its treasure, its pearl. Sorceress of modern times, you have in you both the poison and the antidote, your great power. The Medicine Woman of Healing invites you to find your own medicine. Explore medicinal plants, crystals, dancing, singing, shamanic practices ... Say 'Yes!' to your gift.

⋘ AWAKEN YOUR MEDICINE ⋙

Connect to this archetype, and prepare yourself for a new stage on the path of healing.

Open your ritual space. Take up your drum or your rattle; find healing mantras, *icaro* chants ... Choose an object to represent your wound, which you will later give back to nature. Light a candle, symbolising the light of your consciousness. Draw a healing circle around you. Call your allies – animals, totems, ancestors or guides – before whom you lay down your wound (such as a betrayal in love, lack of recognition, abandonment or abuse). Visualise your tragedy; honour it. Dance, sing and let the tears flow. Close the ritual with a sensory meditation with larch essential oil, a powerful healer. Close the circle. Give thanks.

Find a time to go out in nature to bury the symbol/object you had chosen to represent your wound. You can also call upon a shaman or healer to help you in your rebirth.

'Trust in the process, and enter into the cycle of life, death and rebirth.'

IX. ALL POTENTIALITIES

I OPEN THE DANCE OF SYNCHRONICITIES.

⫷⫷ MESSAGE ⫸⫸

I am the Medicine Woman of All Potentialities. I connect you to the field of universal consciousness, so you may become who you are meant to be. When you resonate with the Great Sacred Dream all ways and means are given to you, so you may smoothly make your projects a reality. With all my love, I present you with the keys of the law of attraction, so you may access the secrets of the universe. Join me in the dance of synchronicities; they show the way at every moment. My secret is this: setting intentions in the service of positive change is your responsibility; you must show goodwill. Then, magic can begin to manifest ...

⫷⫷⫷ GUIDANCE ⫸⫸⫸

The time has come to become your potential. The Medicine Woman of All Potentialities opens you to other, unknown dimensions. Behind our seen and tangible world there is another reality, which you are now ready to explore. Do not worry about how you will attain your goals; solutions will appear as synchronicities present themselves. Have fun; do something new. Trust in the flow, and the universe will co-create with you. What do you really want? Beams of energy converge where you set your intention. Remember: all is potential!

⫷⫷⫷ AWAKEN YOUR MEDICINE ⫸⫸⫸

Connect to this archetype so it may support you and inspire your wish.

Open your ritual space. The practice of *sankalpa* (stemming from the Hindu tradition), or power of attention, involves focusing on a solemn vow or goal with determination. Light a candle, symbolising the flame of your consciousness. Take up your drum, and let a chant of gratitude rise up inside you. Set your sankalpa: what do you really want – to find true love, your dream job, a place where you can rest and recuperate? Be specific: it is for your greater good and is connected to the Great Sacred Dream. With both your hands flat on your belly and your powerful roots deployed into the womb of Mother Earth, plant your wish like a seed in the fertile earth of your uterus. Visualise the details of your wish. Let divine will do its work. Ask for synchronicities to guide you on the path. Blow out your candle, and give thanks.

'For 21 days, water your wish with joy and trust, collect the coincidences in a notebook and embrace your expansion.'

X. DIVINE SENSUALITY

X
DIVINE SENSUALITY
I REVEAL YOUR TALENT TO ENCHANT.

I REVEAL YOUR TALENT TO ENCHANT.

⋘ MESSAGE ⋙

I am the goddess of love, sensuality and desire. Pleasure is
a doorway to carnal celebration, the gift of our incarnation.
I hold the power of sensations, love and creativity. I am
the enchantress, the muse of poets, the lover. My spirit is
the honey of life and catalyst of your talents. I am Venus,

Aphrodite and Shakti. The promise of the marriage of yin and yang resonates in me, and my dances call for sacred union. When you surrender to your impulse of life, you also tap into wonderful inspiration for sublime divine creations.

«« GUIDANCE »»

The time has come to reconnect to your desires, the joy of living and sensuality. 'Treat yourself,' whispers the medicine woman. 'Develop a connection to sacred sensuality.' Like Venus emerging from foaming water in a seashell, let your beauty shine. Celebrate your body, the vehicle of your divine feminine essence and container of your creations. Reconnect to water, the symbol of sensuality, and fertilise your talents. Let yourself be exalted by love and powerfully sensual relationships. Reconnect with your loving and erotic nature. And exalt your creativity in all areas.

«« AWAKEN YOUR MEDICINE »»

Connect to this archetype to reveal your talent to enchant and open the doors of voluptuousness and divine creation.

Open your ritual space. Create an altar dedicated to your divinity. Gather your Venusian objects – seashells, a pink candle, ylang-ylang essential oil and ripe and tasty fruit. Convey your intention to celebrate your divine temple, your desire to live and create. Choose inspiring sensual and erotic music. Take the time to adorn your body with jewels and accessories, as well as make-up, creams and perfume. Celebrate your beauty before a mirror and begin to dance. Undulate; kindle the flame of your cauldron. Let the energy rise up your spine and fill your heart; your arms are arabesques. Improvise; let your vibrant, sensual and voluptuous femininity spread its wings.

'Express your creativity. Give thanks.'

XI. PERSONAL POWER

XI
PERSONAL POWER
I ENCOURAGE YOU TO BE THE MASTER OF YOUR DESTINY.

I ENCOURAGE YOU TO BE THE MASTER OF YOUR DESTINY.

⋘ MESSAGE ⋙

I am the Medicine Woman of Personal Power, and I release all memories of submission. My gift is woman's great power, which is located in her belly, where the seeds of the Great Sacred Dream are nested and where her children come to life. In women's hearts burns the sacred fire, which they need to promote their talents and knowledge. I am she who gives you the courage and boldness to live the life you truly want, not the life others expect you to lead. With me at your side, you will awaken your potential for growth to unfurl your creative energy. You are the master of your destiny.

≪≪ GUIDANCE ≫≫

The time has come to rise up and take your rightful place. The medicine woman benevolently asks you: is there a situation in which you over-adapt? Is there someone to whom you cede your power? You run the real risk of not living your own life. You don't need anyone else's approval. Be bold: be who you truly are, develop your talents and act! Commit to holding aloft your values: peace, truth and the planet's conservation. You are supported: move forward in the full presence of your soul's qualities and validate your choices.

≪≪ AWAKEN YOUR MEDICINE ≫≫

Connect to this archetype, and decide now to take back your personal power.

Open your ritual space. Light a candle. Take up your drum. Outline your personal space by drawing a protective circle around you. Set a talisman before you that gives you strength.

Visualise the situation, or the person to whom you have given your power. Let the emotions come – anger, sadness, powerlessness ... Breathe in cinnamon essential oil, for boldness. Call upon your talent, your leadership. With your talisman, dance to affirm yourself. Be proud of who you are. Then, sit down and feel the energy of feminine power, of the belly, within you. Give thanks, and close the circle.

'You are a woman standing tall. Step forward without waiting to speak; make your voice heard!'

XII. SACRED CEREMONIES

XII
SACRED CEREMONIES
I REMIND YOUR SOUL OF THE SACREDNESS OF THE WORLD

I REMIND YOUR SOUL OF THE SACREDNESS OF THE WORLD.

⟪⟪ MESSAGE ⟫⟫

I am the Medicine Woman of Sacred Ceremonies. I sing ancestral alliances to your soul. Feel my benevolent presence by your side, and celebrate with me the rituals and prayers that keep the world sacred. I am she who brings you the blessing of the spirit that connects all things. I know the power of singing, dancing and healing circles. My drum beats in time with Mother Earth's heart; join me and remember that life is a gift to be celebrated, whatever has been sent to you to experience: births or deaths. My promise is to protect the sacred and secret nature of life, so enchanted harmony may manifest.

⪻ GUIDANCE ⪼

The time has come to gratefully honour the sacredness of all things. Do you feel this miracle unfolding inside and around you? The medicine woman invites you to let yourself be moved by the gift of life, including its hardships, for each trial holds a meaning to be revealed with time. 'Make ritual, pray, dance, sing and give thanks,' whispers the medicine woman benevolently. Re-enchant the ordinary world. What do you have to celebrate: a seasonal passage, birthday, love, hardship overcome, the closing of a cycle, renewal? Whatever it is, honouring this passage will bring you joy, help, comfort or a transformational process.

⪻ AWAKEN YOUR MEDICINE ⪼

Connect to this archetype and discover the power of prayer, which the elders call the 'greatest force in the universe'. The Navajos believe that prayers said to the sound of drums bring inner strength. They give thanks for what already exists and ask the Great Spirit for protection in the days to come. Depending on the tradition, prayer can be a meditation, song for healing or secret vow ... Find your own prayer.

Open a space for prayer. This is a time to connect to subtle planes with a particular intention such as peace, healing or gratitude. In the morning, turn towards Grandfather Sun. Feel his presence and ask him for his blessing over the day for you, your loved ones, your community, your ancestors and all the different realms. In the evening, turn towards Grandmother Moon. Thank her for all you have experienced with profound gratitude and acceptance that all is perfect.

'Considering life with prayers of offering, gratitude and joy is the guiding thread of existence.'

XIII. THE CIRCLE OF LIFE

I GIVE YOU MY BLESSING TO ACCOMPLISH YOUR QUEST.

≪≪ MESSAGE ≫≫

I am the Medicine Woman of the Circle of Life. The tortoise is my totem. Symbol of Mother Earth, the tortoise created the world. Her wisdom underlines the importance of not disturbing the order of things. The divine news is that you have arrived at your destination. My presence indicates an important event: it is time to integrate the different aspects of the deep feminine. The great sacred dream of awakening the feminine has visited your heart. The vision you received is revealing itself and, with it, your personal legend. I offer you my blessing and something of precious help: the medicine wheel, which contains the wise lessons of the progress you've already made and the talents to achieve your quest.

⋘ GUIDANCE ⋙

You are about to finish a cycle, and deep change is happening. Holding aloft the banner of love and truth; you have remained loyal to the song of your soul for this journey into healing the feminine. The medicine woman honours your courage, your humility in diving into your shadows and your pride in revealing your light. You have discovered your own medicine. Honour this gift that has been given to you without delay. You are under my protection, daughter of Gaia. I leave you the wisdom of time immemorial as your inheritance.

≪≪ AWAKEN YOUR MEDICINE ≫≫

Connect to this archetype, and practise the medicine wheel of the 12 archetypes to honour each of your qualities and insights.

Open your ritual space. Place the 12 medicine women cards down on the ground in a circle. With your drum, walk the wheel, stopping before each card. Revisit the various aspects of your femininity. Feel the progress you have made, your unity, your power ...

'This is a time for celebration. Sit down in the centre of the circle. Let a song rise up inside you; feel the presence of the tortoise offering you her unconditional support. Give thanks.'

GIFTS OF THE
FEMININE CARDS

The oracle proposes a maiden quest to discover the gifts of the feminine – values and qualities inherent to women that we need to rehabilitate and experiment the power of. These are the 12 talents of our feminine essence, our *anima*. They are the yin aspect of the wheel, an inner journey.

1. INTUITION

INTUITION IS THE MESSENGER OF YOUR DESTINY; FOLLOW IT!

⊙ MESSAGE ⊙

I am intuition. Like the cat, my Ancient Egyptian totem, I cannot be controlled. I just know!

A precious gift of the feminine soul, intuition offers the keys to our inner world to safely guide our steps.

Considered as our sixth sense, intuition is the complement of reason and allows us to comprehend reality in a different way. This 'irrational function of the psyche', as analyst C.G. Jung put it, can be thought of as a gateway between our inner knowledge and the world around us. Our culture and way of life do not necessarily let us listen to our intuition but, when we follow it, we gain new insight into our lives and are better able to bring luck on our side. Intuition is the primordial resource of the feminine, enabling solutions to appear as if by magic.

⊙ GUIDANCE ⊙

Listen, daughter of the stars and Gaia: the world is speaking to you, sending signs your way. Intuition is your surest compass to guide your steps towards your destiny.

You are intuitive; it is your true nature, so trust in yourself … You might not always pay enough attention to it, but your intuition sends you signs. Ask questions, and listen to the world around you. The universe is full of information: clouds in the sky, conversations and encounters. It is time to take the ways less travelled, as signposted by your intuition, and inspire happy coincidences. Life will unveil its fabulous design for you. Intuition is life's messenger; follow it!

☉ AWAKEN YOUR GIFT ☉

It is time to open up your vision and pay attention to your intuition.

Intuition practice. Take a moment to prepare a clear question about a situation or person and decode your intuitive messages. Look upon your environment with new eyes, as if you were discovering it for the first time. Wherever you are, become an observer; let yourself be drawn to a particular object or person that will provide you with information. Mobilise all your senses to 'see' the signs behind appearances and listen for answers. You may be drawn to a cushion or painting; your ear catches snippets of a conversation … Join the dots.

Intuition also uses specific sensory channels. These can be bodily sensations, such as damp hands or a tight stomach; visual sensations, such as flashes; or auditory sensations, such as your inner voice. Discover your own specific sensory channel and cultivate your intuition. This is the best way to bring new meaning into your life.

2. THE WILD FEMININE

AWAKEN YOUR SHE-WOLF INSTINCT,
THAT PRIMORDIAL FORCE.

⊙ MESSAGE ⊙

I am the wild nature of the feminine. Poet, lover and
mother, I dance in the woods; I create; I thunder; I love with
passion. I am here to walk in your footsteps …

The 'wild feminine' refers to our instinctive force in the service of life. Wildness, that primordial resource of the essence of the feminine, evokes what has not been tamed, conditioned or hemmed in. Clarissa Pinkola Estés reminds us that 'A healthy woman is much like a wolf: robust, chock-full, strong life force, life-giving, territorially aware, inventive, loyal, roving.'[1] Wildness is the foundation of the feminine. An ancestral medicine, it is the mystery of our roots and dreams, of the seen and unseen. By looking deeply inside who we are, we can give to ourselves what we never stop looking for outside ourselves, most often in vain! Rehabilitating the wild woman within us will help us access greater freedom to truly exist, starting with releasing ourselves from a patriarchal system.

⊙ GUIDANCE ⊙

You are a wild woman; have you forgotten? It seems that, to make a place for yourself in this world, you have let yourself be domesticated. A feeling of profound nostalgia – the desire to run with wolves once more – probably floats in your consciousness. It is time to reconnect with your instinctive nature, to open the thousand eyes of your intuition, to summon the ancient histories, to give life. Remember your roots, your cycles, your ties to nature –

1. *Translator's note:* Clarissa Pinkola Estés, *Women Who Run With the Wolves: Myths and Stories of the Wild Woman Archetype*, Ballantine Books, 1992.

all essential to your well-being – to play, love, create and bring shine to your fur once more …

⊙ AWAKEN YOUR GIFT ⊙

Connecting with your wild nature brings you home and invites you to dive into your depths, into your roots. Be bold; contact this primordial force, and follow its healthy wisdom.

Loba ritual. Connect with the she-wolf residing inside your belly close to your ovaries. Take up your drum and rub a drop of vetiver essential oil inside your wrists. Let a scene of vast nature come to you, and open all your senses wide. Call the four elements: air, earth, fire and water. You and Mother Earth are one. Let the moon rise in the coming night of your vision. Call the Loba, Baba Yaga, your wildness. Dance and sing. Ask the Loba for a message. What do you need? What medicine does she have for you? Receive and embrace it. Then, put down your drum and thank the Loba. Write down the messages you have received in your notebook.

3. SACRED SEXUALITY

⊙ 3 ⊙
SACRED SEXUALITY
RECONNECT WITH THE SOURCE OF YOUR DIVINE SEXUALITY

RECONNECT WITH THE SOURCE OF YOUR DIVINE SEXUALITY.

⊙ MESSAGE ⊙

I am kundalini, the snake coiled at the base of your spine, the energy of the deeps, your precious ally for sacred sexuality. The ancient matriarchal tribes worshipped women as cosmic wombs filled with earth's life force. In the orgasmic union of the male and female principles, the delicious beat that moves the elements could express itself. Sexuality, the doorway to true love, thus becomes the prelude to spiritual experiences. In the Hindu tantra tradition, when kundalini awakens our sexual energy rises up the length of our spines, and the bodily aspect fades away before a vast feeling of completeness where heart and consciousness open wide!

⊙ GUIDANCE ⊙

Do you hear the call of your libido? There are paths other than the simple sexual meeting of bodies. This card opens the way of sacred sexuality towards the union of the male and female principles, Shiva and Shakti, bringing you to ecstasy. Be bold, and initiate your partner into this mystery to take your relationship beyond ordinary sexuality. If you are single, reconnect with the source of your divine sexuality; your body is a temple of love. Pleasure is your birthright.

⊙ AWAKEN YOUR GIFT ⊙

In the tantric tradition, sexuality experienced with awareness rests on the sacred dimension of our sexual organs. Tantra considers the yoni, the female sexual organ, to be the doorway to the Great Mystery and connected to a manifestation of Devi, the Great Goddess. This part of the body is worshipped as the source of all life and the hearth of cosmic energy.

Yoni ritual. Sit down in a comfortable position. Close your eyes and become aware of your breath. Now, imagine you can breathe inside your yoni. Feel its expansion when you breathe in, and a light contraction when you breathe out. Become aware of the sensations you feel in your yoni. The point is not to feel aroused, but to connect to your yoni through your breathing. As long as nothing is forced, the energy of kundalini can become awakened with practice.

4. MOTHER EARTH

FORGE A NEW ALLIANCE WITH NATURE.

☉ MESSAGE ☉

Can you hear my song, beloved daughter? I am here, all around you – in the streams, drops of rain, light of the sun and trees that offer you their shade.

Women and Pachamama, our planet, have forged an alliance stretching back to our beginnings. Women have always adapted their lifestyle to the rhythms of nature, the seasons, the course of the moon and cycles of the tides, in keeping with the harmony of the world. When we act against this flow our attitudes provoke imbalances, taking us away from a natural and fulfilling life. The crones say that the day women listen to their own earth, their uterus, which enables them to carry children and holds the seeds of tomorrow's world, they will manifest the Great Sacred Dream. Earth, women's wombs, giving life, dreams ... all are sacred ties to Mother Earth, the Great Mystery of life.

⊙ GUIDANCE ⊙

You are one with Mother Nature. You are water, earth, fire and air. By forging ties with your terrestrial habitat, you can strengthen the foundations of your inner home. When you are in carnal contact with nature's wildness, your skin becomes alive and life beats inside you once more. Can you feel it? In contrast, losing this connection can be revealed through tiredness or lack of trust in yourself and the future. You are not separated. You are not alone. Trust in your own ability to grow, just like Mother Nature all around you. You can count on the life forces inside you!

☉ AWAKEN YOUR GIFT ☉

Go towards Mother Nature and, step by step, forge ties with her as you would with a dear friend. Today, take a walk in nature to meet her intimately.

Ritual of reconnection to Pachamama. Using a rattle, your drum or just your loving heart, go and meet the nature spirits in the stones, moss, breezes, streams or trees. Open up the field of your perceptions to feel their presence. Be silent to listen to their message, their song. Open your eyes wide to see their dance and the light's beauty. Feel and embrace. Then, give thanks by making an offering to that place with fruit, seeds or what you find there.

5. MYSTERY

OPEN YOURSELF UP TO THE UNSEEN;
A DIRECTION IS REVEALED.

☉ MESSAGE ☉

I am a mystery to be experienced, not a problem to solve.
Destiny or providence: open yourself up to this in-between
realm.

While society encourages us to rationalise, let's return to mystery! Beyond their multiple daily occupations and commitments, women possess an ability and taste for mystery, for myths and legends. They know the power of the great archetypes that rule us, and can see beyond appearances. Unseen worlds are familiar to us, whether they be the realms of ancestors, spirit guides, animal people, planets or even the deceased. The dance of the cosmos is a language that we aspire to decode.

⊙ GUIDANCE ⊙

Life whispers to you; there is a reality beyond what we see. To discover that other reality, it is time to open yourself up to other dimensions and cultivate a new intimacy with the world. This card questions your life path. Leave your certainties aside. Change your outlook. Listen to hidden meanings, to the world between realms. Mystery can then present itself and offer you a new understanding of your life pattern and all its threads ... between destiny and providence. Lift the veil. Don't try to find ready-made solutions. A realisation, a direction, will be revealed to you!

⊙ AWAKEN YOUR GIFT ⊙

Somewhere inside you there is the memory of ancestral wisdom, a memory that knows the magic of life.

Summon the medicine of the unseen, the source of the feminine. There are different ways to converse with the universe – the science of archetypes, stories, runes and dreams. Go and meet them to answer your question. You can also draw a medicine wheel, or consult the planets with the help of an astrologer. Engage in a practice that meets your soul's aspiration. What is your medium? Question and explore. Let yourself be initiated by the great adventure of life ... Then meaning will appear, unveiling your destiny.

6. SELF-KNOWLEDGE

DIVE INTO YOUR DEPTHS, WHERE YOUR TRUTH RESIDES.

☉ MESSAGE ☉

I am the memory of your divine nature. I breathe into you
the powerful desire for inner quests, the light on the path
to self-knowledge.

Enveloped in the veils of their femininity, women are able to retire within themselves in their caves. Interiority is a woman's nature ... Deep inside that space out of time, where past and future meet, women affirm their taste for inner journeys. They know that to build the foundations of their homes, to align with who they truly are, they must take a risk: to encounter the deep levels of their psyche. That is where a woman discovers the intimate truth of her universe, the truth that rules her own cosmogony, which is connected to the cosmogony of the world.

⊙ GUIDANCE ⊙

You are a woman of knowledge. It is time to shine a light on the true nature of who you are. To start on this journey towards yourself you will have to dive into the depths of your unconscious. Do so gently. To face your unconscious is the first step towards healing. Shed light on your shadows; collect your experiences then sieve them through your inner vision. You can consult a therapist or a shaman, or carry out a ritual. Once you begin your individual inner revolution, you can change the world.

⊙ AWAKEN YOUR GIFT ⊙

To undertake this journey, retire from the noise of the world so you can hear the melody of your own story. Make time to meet with yourself.

Ritual of intentional solitude that reveals who you are to yourself. Draw a symbolic circle around yourself to open the doors to your inner being. Then, let an inspiring vision of a comforting cave come to you. Savour this contact with your presence, alone. Ask questions in the silence of your interiority. What secrets, what resources, does your unconscious harbour in connection with this situation? Go and look for a treasure chest. Open it, and find an object! Receive the information and let it disappear into a cloud of butterflies, symbols of transformation. Come back here and now, inside the room.

To continue this inner dialogue, perform a self-knowledge practice by writing down your insights in your notebook. Commit to making time to reconnect with yourself regularly.

7. EMOTIONS

EMOTIONS

YOU ARE AN EMOTIONAL CREATURE; FERTILISE THAT GREAT POWER

YOU ARE AN EMOTIONAL CREATURE; FERTILISE THAT GREAT POWER!

⊙ MESSAGE ⊙

I am your precious ally, the infinite and whimsical range of your emotions, the memory of your feelings, the spice of your creative and relational life.

Our western civilisation has fostered intellect and rationality, but has neglected the emotional side of life ... and of women, who are emotional creatures par excellence. We distrust the emotional realm, which is such a pity! Our darling emotions (joy, sadness, anger ...) are intelligent movements of the body. Even more so than our physiological integrity, they contribute to our psychological well-being. Emotions are also intimately connected to our memory; they are essential to our social lives and even more to our creativity. A fabulous gift, they should be honoured.

⊙ GUIDANCE ⊙

This card gives you permission to express your emotions freely – to exult, rebel, burst out laughing or sing and dance your sadness. Perhaps you still need to struggle, keep your emotions in check and conform to the expectations of society, the people around you and your partner. It is time to fertilise your world, your psyche, and remedy a form of dryness. Your emotions are the creative salt of your feminine nature; release them before they burst into your life uninvited.

☉ AWAKEN YOUR GIFT ☉

Emotions are connected to the watery aspect of the feminine, a psychological catalyst for an inventive life. To fertilise this great imaginative power, make time for creative practices.

Water of emotions ritual. Wrap an ocean-coloured shawl around your shoulders, light a blue candle and fill a large ceremonial bowl with water. With both hands immersed in the water, allow your emotional situation to come to you. Remain still, with the water lapping inside the bowl, and let a song, dance, words or tears rise up inside you. Let it flow through you. Then, breathe in fresh ginger essential oil, for emotional balance. Write down a creative action in your notebook, draw something or write a poem or another imaginative idea.

Plan for this ritual in your calendar during your premenstrual time, the most emotional phase of your cycle, to pacify an excess of emotion, whether you are crying for no reason or burning with anger ...

8. YOUR BODY'S POWER

YOUR BODY IS YOURS;
CELEBRATE YOUR TEMPLE.

⊙ MESSAGE ⊙

I am irresistible strength, the doorway to your soul. I am
your temple, your place of power, your loyal messenger!

A woman's body is a complete mystery. A world of
its own, sequenced according to its monthly cycle and

blood, it experiences powerful phases throughout its life – adolescence, maternity, breast-feeding, menopause ... The female body embraces the tumult of pleasure and emotions. Object of desire or powerful ace of seduction, throughout time it has been disgraced or adored, battered or worshipped. Re-appropriating your body is a priority: your body is yours.

⊙ GUIDANCE ⊙

Your life stories have made you who you are; your body carries the memory of taboos as well as pleasures. You have probably experienced the power of your body, released through orgasm and giving birth. This card invites you to love your body resolutely and re-appropriate it. Do you know it well? It is time to trust in your body and reconnect with your uterus, your seat of power. Be sure you are truly on the side of love, banishing all-too-often negative judgements.

⊙ AWAKEN YOUR GIFT ⊙

You are beautiful. Awaken your unknown riches, the power that lives inside each cell of your body, the life flowing through you, carrying pleasure and vitality.

Sensory practice. Take a moment to connect with your feelings through spontaneous dancing, becoming aware of your perineum or massaging yourself. Call upon the inner knowing that comes from feeling. What do you need? Explore; let yourself be guided. Each new space of freedom gives you new energy and self-love. Glitter with all your sensory majesty! Welcome to your body.

Plan time for a massage, a bath, lovemaking or another fulfilling sensory experience.

9. THE FEMININE CYCLE

9

THE FEMININE CYCLE

RECONNECT WITH YOUR CYCLE; YOU ARE A PLURAL WOMAN.

RECONNECT WITH YOUR MENSTRUAL CYCLE; YOU ARE A PLURAL WOMAN.

☉ MESSAGE ☉

I am the magic of your feminine cycle. I am the plural woman.

A woman's nature is cyclic! Our menstrual cycle is divided into four phases ... Most often reduced to our period, or fertility phases, our cycle is in fact a treasure and source of wisdom to be rediscovered. Our society and lifestyles do not consider the fundamental reality of our thoughts, behaviour and abilities fluctuating over the course of each month. The good news is that we are plural beings – four women, four potentials in one. By changing our outlook on our menstrual cycle, we can transform our entire life.

☉ GUIDANCE ☉

Remember who you are! Step out of linear time to embrace the roundness of your nature. You may have the feeling of going against the flow or being tired. It is time to honour the richness of your feminine cycle and listen to your inner tempo. You are like the course of the moon and the dance of the seasons: each of the four phases has a specific influence on your libido and your fertility, but also your emotions and behaviour. Witch, business woman, lover, mother ... each woman you are in turn carries the potential to connect you to the wider community of women. Discover that potential! This card is also an invitation to pass wisdom down to your daughter.

☉ AWAKEN YOUR GIFT ☉

Honouring your cycle is a way of recognising the magic of your feminine nature. Getting to know that cycle better enables you to discover your talents. According to the model established by life coach Miranda Gray, identify which phase you are currently in – pre-ovulation/dynamic, ovulation/expressive, pre-menstrual/creative or menstruation/contemplative – and dive into that specific energy.

If you are in your moon time, your period, take time to rest, and celebrate this phase by wearing red. You can give your blood back to the earth, symbol of your belonging, or you can join a red tent, a circle in which women gather during their moon times.

If you have reached menopause, connect to the course of the Grandmother Moon (waxing and waning phases) for your projects. According to ancestral traditions, you and she are one.

10. EMBRACE!

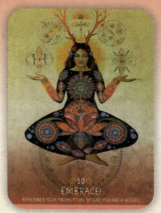

10

EMBRACE!

REMEMBER YOUR PRIMORDIAL NATURE; YOU ARE A VESSEL!

REMEMBER YOUR PRIMORDIAL NATURE; YOU ARE A VESSEL!

☉ MESSAGE ☉

I am the heart cup, symbol of the feminine vessel. Made of curves and hollows, I embrace all forms of life in my belly, my matrix.

A woman is made to embrace, to receive from another. Like her psyche, the shape of her body is made of curves and hollows. And no matter what analyst Sigmund Freud says, a woman does not embrace to fulfil a need but to create something new – that is the female principle! She is a vessel, a matrix ready to be fertilised. A woman's encounter with another aims to create, whether that is a child yet to be born, a work of art, a social project or simply a thing of beauty. Embracing is the doorway to fertility.

☉ GUIDANCE ☉

To obtain your victories, you may have become a fighter, warrior or hyperactive person. Be proud of your successes. However, this card asks a fundamental question: enclosed in armour to be efficient, holding fast to a defensive position, have you cut yourself away from your feelings, the vital source of infinite possibilities? Remember your primordial nature: you are a vessel. You have the ability to be flowed through. It is time to stop struggling, surrender to what is here – to life presenting itself before you, a relationship, project, child … The key word is 'embrace'!

☉ AWAKEN YOUR GIFT ☉

To embrace, you need a receptive attitude.

Embracing practice. Throughout the day, take short moments to let yourself be inspired by the course of life, a word or attitude. Spot those times when you judge, sticking to your position, or when you are defensive. You must somehow let go and surrender! There is nothing passive about surrender; in surrendering, you must look for the creation you sensed in the encounter. Nourishing your taste for otherness is invigorating, and a new space opens in the dance of breathing in and out.

11. THE PATH OF BEAUTY

○ 11 ○
THE PATH OF BEAUTY
WALKING YOUR PATH OF BEAUTY ELEVATES YOUR FEMININE SOUL.

WALKING YOUR PATH OF BEAUTY ELEVATES YOUR FEMININE SOUL.

☉ MESSAGE ☉

I am the spirit of beauty that inspires your poetic soul to embellish the world from day to day. I open the door to wonder at the miracle of life.

In the Navajo tradition, cultivating the 'path of beauty' contributes to keeping *hozho*, the harmony and balance of the world. Each time we are touched by it beauty has a singular impact in our lives, even if we are not always completely aware of it. Depending on who we are, beauty can appease us, give us new courage or put us face to face with mystery, but it will always elevate our soul because its enigma lights up our entire existence. Walking our path of beauty gives us a profound feeling of belonging to the world.

⊙ GUIDANCE ⊙

Beauty gives you a feeling of inner completeness, which nourishes your female principle, bringing you into contemplation and wonder before the grace of the world.

You look for this essential emotion in nature, a person or a place in which you live. You need beauty to feel alive. Beauty allows you to rise, for a time, above the weight of daily conflicts. Then, harmony between the body and mind can emerge, giving you the feeling of being one with the world around you. In that moment of unity, brought to you by beauty, you are reconciled with your own self.

⊙ AWAKEN YOUR GIFT ⊙

Commit to caring for beauty as a truly feminist act.

Beauty practice. Make time to go out and delight in the beauty of nature – before a graceful tree standing alone in a field, the ocean lapping on white sand or a mountain reaching for the sky. Ground yourself in the feeling of harmony, and let yourself be enveloped by beauty. Keep your eyes wide open: it can happen in a museum, but also in the street. In your daily life, see how you can embellish each instant, creating beauty and restoring the harmony of the world through song, a mandala or another form of inspiration.

12. THE HEART'S WISDOM

LISTEN TO THE CALL OF YOUR HEART, YOUR GUIDE IN LOVE.

⊙ MESSAGE ⊙

I envelop you in the gentleness of my love, and spread a healing balm over your heart so you may find, once again, the courage to love.

Ancestral traditions show that the heart is the centre of profound wisdom. The Cherokee language has a term for it: *chante ishta*, or the 'one and only eye of the heart'. Among the Omaha people of North America it is said, 'Ask from the heart and you will be answered from the heart.' Women are the keepers of this cup, or grail, inspired by the unconditional love of Mother Earth, Grandfather Sun and Grandmother Moon.

Far deeper than a romantic trifle, the heart is our ultimate recourse for a vibrant life. Today, we need to make the choice of love.

☉ GUIDANCE ☉

Remember your true nature. Love is a precious treasure nestled in the depths of your heart that you may have buried or covered in armour through the hardships you have encountered along the way. Remember: there is no rose without thorns yet true love is your only way, the song of your heart, your guide. The time has come once again to experience love and become loving in your relationship with your partner, loved ones or spirituality. There are many ways to open the doors of love, such as empathy, compassion and kindness, to bring it into ourselves.

☉ AWAKEN YOUR GIFT ☉

Love is an inner revolution; it begins with loving yourself. Love is like a flower that blooms under a gentle daily light of kindness and exhales its perfume into its surroundings.

Olfactory meditation. Using damask rose essential oil, a healing balm for the heart, dab a few drops inside your wrists and breathe in. Imagine you are in a rose garden, and let yourself be enveloped in benevolent and loving energy. Feel your resistances melt and loving light shine from your heart. Then, join your hands in prayer, and chant *'Dum'*, the bija mantra of the Hindu goddess Durga, famed for her loving power. Give thanks.

The next step is to offer your considerate attention to someone in your family, or a colleague, stranger on the bus or anyone else, at some point during the day.

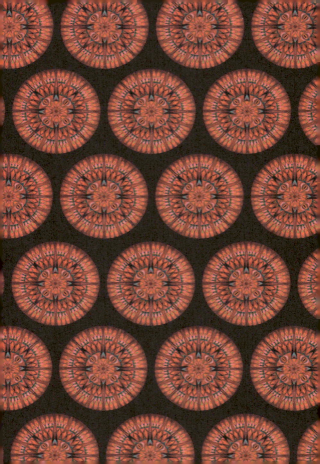

TOTEMS/ALLIED SPIRITS CARDS

In shamanism, all is circle. The medicine wheel represents the universe, or the 'great all' that contains all things. The medicine wheel is divided into four sections, corresponding to the four cardinal points – north, south, east and west. Each cardinal point is usually associated with a season, animal and element (earth, water, fire and air). Each totem, or allied spirit, carries a specificity that the shamans call 'medicine power' – a force they will pass on to you.

13. BISON TOTEM

13
BISON TOTEM
LIFE IS SHOWERING YOU WITH ITS ABUNDANCE.

LIFE IS SHOWERING YOU WITH ITS ABUNDANCE.

I am the spirit of the bison. I ensure you will want for nothing. Emblem of winter, I bring you my support in tough times.

ᐱᐧᐱ SYMBOLISM ᐱᐧᐱ

Keeper of the northern door, the bison shows the way towards the sharing and giving of ourselves. He reminds us that this is a world of abundance, and teaches us to be satisfied with what we already have. Life is generous. The bison teaches us to appreciate our resources and use what we need respectfully. Traditionally, tribes honoured this sacred animal that provided for them with its skin, meat, ligaments and bones. The bison carries the spirit of community; together, we are stronger.

His message. Show respect for and gratitude towards life. In return, life will give you everything you need, in abundance.

ᐱᐧᐱ GUIDANCE ᐱᐧᐱ

When the bison appears in a reading, it is for you to question your relationship with life. The bison invites you to become aware of the abundance around you. Everything is already here, right at your fingertips. You may be experiencing a time of shortage that worries you. By showing greater gratitude for what you already have (such as family, friends and material possessions), you will find a new balance and the ability to honour life. By showing generosity, you will initiate a virtuous cycle. Develop your inner riches and find your community; the medicines of the bison are solidarity and empathy.

⁂ CONTACT YOUR ANIMAL GUIDE ⁂

Reaffirm your trust in life and its generosity to nourish a deep feeling of abundance.

Cornucopia ritual. Call upon the bison spirit guide to reawaken your feeling of prosperity. Gather elements that symbolise your riches – photographs of your family, friends and parties; gifts you have received; objects you love. Add fruit, vegetables and seeds, totem flowers of nature's generosity. Create a mandala, and go into its centre. Feel how life showers you with its blessings! Then, ask your questions. What can you give to your community? How can you be generous? Open your arms; you are ready to give and receive. The bison is a great teacher of generosity. To close the ritual, say a prayer of gratitude and thank the spirit of the bison. In your notebook, write down the messages you have received.

14. EAGLE TOTEM

14
EAGLE TOTEM
RISE ABOVE TO WIDEN YOUR VISION

RISE ABOVE TO WIDEN YOUR VISION.

I am the spirit of the eagle. I remind you that, by rising above, you acquire a new and more spiritual point of view. Trust in your spirit.

⋀⋀⋀ SYMBOLISM ⋀⋀⋀

Keeper of the eastern door, the eagle is a messenger of creative spirit. He possesses the precious ability to fly up high to see clearly. Associated with the element of air, the eagle is majesty, but also a great warrior. He carries the qualities of vision and determination, which are indispensable to walking our spiritual path. An eagle's feather is a badge of honour, a sign of wisdom.

His message. You are a spiritual being in a physical body; spirit is everywhere. It is time to connect the material to the spiritual.

⁂ GUIDANCE ⁂

When the eagle appears in a reading it is to invite you to widen your vision and acquire a new perspective. You may be assailed by worries of daily life weighing on you, and are unable to see the bigger picture. Spread your wings; fly high. The celestial world is speaking to you. Sometimes, you need to leave gravity behind to feel the winds of freedom blowing through your life. You are much more than you think you are. Reconnect with your majesty and talk to the great winds, which entrust you with the keys of your destiny … Take flight!

⁂ CONTACT YOUR ANIMAL GUIDE ⁂

Reaffirm your connection with divine realms for your material life, and rise above.

Feather ritual. Call upon the eagle spirit guide to receive messages from the Great Spirit. Pick up a feather with your left hand and connect to the skies. Consider your question clearly: where would you like some insight? On what issue would you like a new perspective? Honour the element of air, the eagle's symbol; breathe in deeply and fill your lungs. Feel yourself becoming lighter; space is opening up between your shoulder blades. Your wings are spreading out … and your spirit takes flight to the skies above. You are carried effortlessly on the air. Call for a wider vision and embrace the images that come to you. To close the ritual, say a prayer of gratitude and thank the spirit of the eagle. In your notebook, write down the messages you have received.

15. BEAR TOTEM

15
BEAR TOTEM
RETIRE INTO YOUR DEN TO FIND ANSWERS

RETIRE INTO YOUR DEN
TO FIND ANSWERS.

I am the spirit of the bear. I invite you to retire from the world into your den ... to take some time alone. I am the time of dreams, hibernation and rest.

ᚖᚙᚖ SYMBOLISM ᚖᚙᚖ

Keeper of the western door, the bear retires into his cave to observe a time for dreams. Once regenerated, he feeds and exercises his great power. His clan is one of leaders and healers. His totem is connected to the earth, and he is respected for his strength and power; he is a born leader. In some traditions, the bear is associated with rites of initiation, aiming to awaken to a new state of consciousness. The bear is the ancestor and, as such, he is venerated.

His message. Your inner strength is powerful. Remember, whatever you experience, light always shines in the darkness. Dive into yourself.

ᚖᚙᚖ GUIDANCE ᚖᚙᚖ

When the bear appears in a reading it is to invite you to take a break, to escape from the world and dive into your den, your interiority. Doubtlessly, you need some rest to renew your energies. There is no point in running around to try to change a situation or move it forward. A great dream slumbers inside you, and it needs silence to emerge. Something new is trying to become a reality. A time out alone is necessary. During that time you will receive earth's breath of power, and you will be able to summon your natural leadership once more.

⁂ CONTACT YOUR ANIMAL GUIDE ⁂

Honour your need for inner silence, a time of introspection, and find the answers within yourself.

She-bear cave ritual. Call upon the she-bear spirit guide, and plan for some hibernation time with the she-bear cave ritual – called a *tiowé* in the Native American tradition, meaning a time of stillness and silence. For an hour, sit in darkness in your room in warmth and cosiness, with a comforting drink and dried fruit. Take up your drum and enter into your dream space. Let a song dedicated to the she-bear rise up inside you, and navigate this in-between. Find your path and call its qualities. Let visions come to you. Savour this time of intentional solitude. To close the ritual, say a prayer of gratitude and thank the spirit of the she-bear. In your notebook, write down the messages you have received.

You can also find a spot in nature for this ritual, or go for a short retreat.

16. COYOTE TOTEM

SHOW HUMOUR; LAUGHTER IS YOUR MEDICINE.

I am the spirit of the coyote, the sacred clown. I bring you the medicine of laughter, so you can take a step back and laugh at yourself. I tease and destabilise you so you may find unknown resources inside yourself.

⁂ SYMBOLISM ⁂

Keeper of the southern door, the coyote is also called the 'sacred dog' in native traditions. His presence is associated with wiliness, and is not always welcomed. His totem is destabilising; he hides deep wisdom in what can look like trickery or a bad joke from the universe. What can seem negative or chaotic can conceal hidden truth. The coyote's presence is often troubling. He is a powerful teacher who gives you the opportunity to move away from excessively rigid seriousness and be more cheerful.

His message. Don't take the situation too seriously; cultivate humour and the message will be revealed to you.

⁂ GUIDANCE ⁂

When the coyote appears in a reading, it is to encourage you to show greater humour … You may feel someone is playing you, but you don't need to make a big deal of it. Instead, try to open your mind to the incongruous. Change your point of view, now. The coyote can also point to a form of self-sabotage; perhaps you have fallen back into bad habits. If you are facing disappointments or setbacks, laughter will help effect change more easily. The coyote's presence also invites you to check whether you might be deceiving yourself, telling stories to yourself.

⁂ CONTACT YOUR ANIMAL GUIDE ⁂

Reconnect with the ability to laugh at yourself, and bring things down to a lower key. Show a little weirdness to get through disorder and contrary winds.

Laughter ritual. Call upon the coyote spirit guide, and leave seriousness behind. Learn to laugh at yourself; develop a farcical view of the situation or your flaws. Take up an accessory that symbolises and exaggerates the situation to awaken your inner clown. Climb up on a chair like being on stage, and tell your story as if you were a stand-up comedian before an audience.

Let yourself get caught up in the game. Get off your pedestal, and have some fun. Perform a laughter yoga practice. If you let your breath come in gasps, shaking up your diaphragm, your body will contract and produce waves of laughter. Laugh, and then laugh some more. Never mind if your laughter is inauthentic; the important thing is to benefit from its tremors and free your solar plexus. There, you see: it's not that hard. You have just stepped back from the drama. Take a deep breath. Thank the spirit of the coyote. Start over again as many times as necessary; the hidden teaching or new solutions will appear.

17. SPIRIT OF FIRE

SPIRIT OF FIRE
SHINE YOUR POWER, UNRESERVEDLY

SHINE YOUR POWER, UNRESERVEDLY.

~▲~ **MESSAGE** ~▲~

I am the spirit of fire, the creative principle. I am fire, gifted
to humans by Prometheus to protect them from darkness.
I am the spirit of west on the medicine wheel. I am the will-
o'-the-wisps in fireplaces, bringing warmth to your bones
and soul. I am the fire in the sky, lighting up the night with

my power, declaring my love to Mother Earth with a stroke of sublime lightning. I am the volcano, awakening together with your inner fire. I am light, the vibrant flame of your consciousness and candles, memories of your prayers. I am the fire of your libido, pulsating in your belly, the source of life and desire. I burn at midsummer against all prohibitions, revealing your ardent nature.

⋀⋁⋀ GUIDANCE ⋀⋁⋀

This card invites you to awaken your fire, your powerful impulse of life. In times past, a flame burned constantly in the temple of the Moon Goddess, the essence of the feminine. Become that flame, light of fertility, once more. If you feel any doubts or the urge to give up, shine the light of your consciousness unreservedly, and declare victory over the shadows. The Spirit of Fire in your reading also means it is time to rekindle the flame of burning desire, celebrating your life energy once more and saying 'Yes' to pleasure.

⋀⋁⋀ AWAKEN THE MEDICINE ⋀⋁⋀

Call the spirit of fire to support you. What message is fire bringing you? To find out, dedicate a moment to this spirit.

At home. Perform a ritual to shine your power. Light two candles, one representing your fertilising power and the other holding the flame of purification that removes all obstacles. Invoke the spirit of fire, entrusting it with your wish. Write down on a piece of paper every thought limiting that wish. Burn the paper. Then, write a poem celebrating your talents. Give thanks. Display the poem in a light-filled spot.

In nature. Offer yourself to the warmth of the sun, and feel how it warms your three hearths – the fires in your belly, heart and consciousness. Awaken the solar woman ... and say a prayer for her.

18. SPIRIT OF AIR

18
SPIRIT OF AIR
A FAVOURABLE WIND IS BLOWING ON YOUR LIFE.

A FAVOURABLE WIND IS BLOWING ON YOUR LIFE.

⁂ MESSAGE ⁂

I am the spirit of air; I am breath. Fresh or warm against your nose, when I entered your lungs I was your first cry. I fill the sails of ships to navigate the fabulous oceans of your life. I am movement. Trade wind, breeze, zephyr or sirocco, I imbue each patch of your land with the taste of my breath. I am the resource of your phenomenal flight towards a light-filled destiny. I am the dance of ferns in the depths of the forest, and I release the superfluous from your life. Unseen yet present everywhere, I am life.

⋀⋀⋀ GUIDANCE ⋀⋀⋀

This card invites you to play with air and taste the joy of lightness. Be like a feather, listening to your divine resonance, where light glitters. Be like a leaf, letting itself get caught up in dancing upon the wind's invitation. Let go. Perhaps you feel weighed down by a situation, relationship or place, with a heaviness of body or heart. It is time to rise above and spread your wings. The spirit of air in your reading also means that new love or work-related opportunities are presenting themselves; the winds are favourable to you.

⋀⋀⋀ AWAKEN THE MEDICINE ⋀⋀⋀

Call the spirit of air to support you. What message is air bringing you? To find out, dedicate a moment to this spirit.

At home. Perform a ritual for increased lightness. Open your windows to air out your living space. Gather a few feathers. Breathe in deeply and feel lightness inside. Invoke the spirit of air, entrusting it with a situation that weighs heavily – your question. Then, throw the feathers in the air above your head, feel your consciousness rise above and take a step back. Embrace new solutions. Give thanks.

In nature. Offer yourself to the wind caressing your skin. Listen to its melody in the trees. Pay attention – leaves dancing in the air, lightness or falling to the ground, letting go. Awaken the bird woman ... and say a prayer for her.

19. SPIRIT OF EARTH

HAVE FAITH; YOU ARE SUPPORTED.

༄ MESSAGE ༄

I am the spirit of earth, Mother Earth, imprinted with the footsteps of her children. Mountain, clearing or desert, I clothe myself in colour to manifest the beauty of life. I am humus, as close to you and your humanity as can be. I am generous and fertile. I am life, in which you can lay down or retire in a cave. The plant world takes root inside me, producing sumptuous forests, prodigious orchards and countless medicinal herbs. I provide shelter to the forest people, and minerals and crystals grow in my breast. I am your carnal principle.

ᚾᚾᚾ GUIDANCE ᚾᚾᚾ

This card reminds you that you are a daughter of Gaia, our primordial mother. She invites you to plunge your roots into her earth to ground yourself and manifest your dreams. Support your health with fruit and vegetables from her body. Medicinal plants and clay are powerful allies for you. Perhaps you are having trouble bringing a project to life or finding your rightful place. The spirit of earth in your reading renews your faith. Reconnect with your inner earth, your uterus, the seat of feminine power. You are safe.

ᚾᚾᚾ AWAKEN THE MEDICINE ᚾᚾᚾ

Call the spirit of earth to support you. What message is earth bringing you? To find out, dedicate a moment to this spirit.

In nature. Perform a grounding ritual. Walk barefoot on earth; listen to the beat of her pulse; plunge your roots into her belly. Invoke the spirit of earth, and entrust it with your request. Pay attention – to ferns rustling, a bird singing, a pattern in the bark of a tree … Become fertile earth for its messages. Symbolise its presence on your altar with an element from nature that will support you. Give thanks.

At home. Take care of your plants; cook with produce harvested from the earth. Take up your drum to connect to earth's heart. Awaken the wild woman … and say a prayer for her.

20. SPIRIT OF WATER

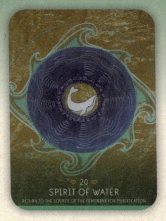

RETURN TO THE SOURCE OF THE FEMININE FOR PURIFICATION.

〰 MESSAGE 〰

I am the spirit of water, the pure source that flows down the mountain. I am Mother Ocean, one with the mystery of beginnings, your birth and the deeps. I am the rock-filled source, the limpid river, the home of the *vouivre*, serpent-women sorceresses, and of nymphs and undines. I am water and I purify you. In the ebb and flow of tides, I unite with Grandmother Moon's cycle to extend my multi-faceted and unpredictable essence. Melodious lapping, froth or waves, lake or impetuous torrent, I am elusive. I am the female principle.

⁂ GUIDANCE ⁂

This card invites you to remember where you came from. Your tears are filled with salt, just like the universal mother. The blood of moon times flows from you to purify you with each cycle, and your breasts gush nourishing milk ... Your nature is oceanic! There can be times when too much activity, being wounded in a love relationship or another emotional trouble can cause your source to dry up. Maybe you need to be more hydrated or to swim in flowing water. The spirit of water in your reading gives you permission to release your emotions to resume the fluid and ringing course of your destiny.

⁂ AWAKEN THE MEDICINE ⁂

Call the spirit of water to support you. What message is water bringing you? To find out, dedicate a moment to this spirit.

At home. Perform a purification ritual with Lemanjá, the goddess of the ocean. According to legend, we can sit before the sea to whisper our worries to her and light a blue candle. Fill a bowl dedicated to your ritual with water and recite Lemanjá's mantra: *'Yemaya Assessu Yemaya yemaya Olodo Olodo yemaya.'* ('Yemaya, welcome me into your ocean.') Once you have entrusted her with your sorrow, immerse your hands in water to purify yourself. Give thanks.

In nature. Connect to the spirit of water. Offer yourself to the rain, swim in a lake or sing on the banks of a stream. Feel its purity, clarity and transparency. Awaken the serpent woman and say a prayer to her.

21. AUTUMN

21
AUTUMN
A TIME FOR LETTING GO; LIGHTEN YOUR LOAD

A TIME FOR LETTING GO;
LIGHTEN YOUR LOAD.

⁂ MESSAGE ⁂

In the Celtic tradition, the autumn equinox symbolises the time of abundance – harvests are at their peak – but also the season during which we need to prepare for austerity. Autumn is a time of descent: warmth and light decline, energy fades. It is a phase of deeply letting go. The season brings with it a double outer/inner movement, a transition. Nature slowly goes to sleep, divesting itself of all that is destined to 'die' to be recycled into humus. She also invites us to let go of what weighs on us or has passed its peak.

⋏⋏ GUIDANCE ⋏⋏

Whatever the season you're in right now, this card indicates a time of transition, of coming home to yourself and letting go. You may have been moving forward at a steady pace, doing your best to respond to external requests. By forging ties with the medicine woman inside you, you can contact your instinctive force and listen to your own rhythms. You need to take stock. Observe! What projects have been crowned with success? What dreams have manifested? It is time to harvest the fruits of your work and stock up for the winter, letting go of what produces nothing – your dead leaves.

⋏⋏ AWAKEN THE MEDICINE ⋏⋏

In an echo of the autumn season and the element of earth associated with it, reconnect to your inner earth, your humus, your rooting. Strengthen your grounding to let go and lighten your load. Become the tree that lets its leaves and nuts fall to the ground. Explore this in-between outer/ inner period, this time of returning to intimacy, and ask yourself: of what do you need to let go, to divest yourself, on the physical plane, but also the psychological or relationship planes? Fear, habits, a relationship … To bring yourself closer to your essential truth, and the nature of who you truly are, your true self.

Give thanks. Make an offering to Mother Earth – a poem, a song or food.

22. WINTER

**A TIME FOR TURNING INWARD;
REST IN SILENCE.**

ᗩᑎ MESSAGE ᗩᑎ

With the winter solstice on 21 December, darkness
reaches its peak, signalling the need to enter the cave
of our interiority. The time has come for listening to our
underground river. It is the 'cold season', as the elders call

it, when the noise of the world goes to sleep and gives way to the sparkling rustle of fairyland. It is the season of fabulous beings from the forests, mountains and rivers bringing protection and joy to the home. Associated with silence and retreat from the world, winter invites us to embrace the cycle of life, death and rebirth ... and opens up the realm of dreams.

⋏⃨ GUIDANCE ⋏⃨

Whatever the season you're in right now, this card indicates a time of rest, of silence. During this period, the world of tomorrow is being created in you. By forging ties with the medicine woman inside you, you can give yourself a time of introspection, an inner journey. A promise of renewal is in the works; an adventure is waiting for you, one that only your heart knows. Strengthen your inner light to illuminate the way ahead, which will be revealed to you. This season is also the time for stories; invoke tales and legends to rekindle the flame of the unseen world ... and of your own roots.

⋏⃨ AWAKEN THE MEDICINE ⋏⃨

In an echo of the winter season and the great silence associated with it, retire into the cave of dreams for a time of inner visions. Light a candle, symbolising your light. Take up your drum (or inspiring music) to bring on an altered state of consciousness. Breathe in frankincense essential oil to connect to your celestial roots. Visualise a sacred cave. Envision your request to the fairy realm: 'Something inside me sleeps in deepest secrecy. Thank you for the visions, your messages.' Let things arise on their own. Write them down in your notebook and, in the days that follow, observe what comes to support your dream.

Give thanks. Make an offering to the fairy realm – a poem, song or candle.

23. SPRING

23
SPRING
A TIME FOR RENEWAL; STEP INTO UNCHARTED TERRITORY.

A TIME FOR RENEWAL; STEP INTO UNCHARTED TERRITORY.

⟩⟩⟩ MESSAGE ⟨⟨⟨

In spring, nature wakes up in a marvellous exuberance of perfume, colour and budding growth. Earth reveals its magnificence. The Celtic tradition celebrates the spring equinox with the goddess Ostara, symbol of life's renewal.

What has been nurtured in the silence of winter can now manifest vitally, dynamically and joyously. The season brings with it a rise in sap; something new wishes to emerge. We witness a rebirth. The promise of growth in the seeds we sowed in the earth and our dreams manifests. This new cycle supports material fulfilment.

GUIDANCE

Whatever the season you're in right now, this card indicates a powerful longing for renewal, much like an irrepressible desire to shake your scales or feathers to bring yourself out of lethargy. Forge ties with the medicine woman inside you, be bold and bravely answer the commanding call of life. An opportunity to reinvent yourself, to innovate, is presenting itself. Seize it. Whether in your work, love or creative life, anything new is favourable to you. Take a fertile leap into uncharted territory.

AWAKEN THE MEDICINE

In an echo of the spring season and the great energy of renewal associated with it, release the old to make place for the new. Make time to perform a cleansing ritual with some burning sage. Plants are at the heart of Ostara celebrations. Standing tall, proceed in three steps.

I ask the sage to:

1. Accompany me in the purification process.
2. Cleanse me of any (physical, emotional, relational) pollution.
3. Bring clarity so the seeds of renewal may grow.

Wave the burning sage stick in circular movements around you, from bottom to top, to envelop yourself in a cylinder of smoke. Sit down, and let the cleansing take place.

Give thanks. Make an offering by putting a packet of seeds (symbol of sowing) or flowers on your altar.

24. SUMMER

24
SUMMER
A TIME FOR BLOOMING; CELEBRATE YOUR SUCCESSES

A TIME FOR BLOOMING;
CELEBRATE YOUR SUCCESSES.

⚞ MESSAGE ⚟

In the Celtic tradition, the summer solstice is celebrated on 21 June, the longest night of the year. The ceremonies provide a time to give thanks for what has been given, and prepare us to embrace what is coming. Life is in full swing of sunlight, the flutter of butterfly wings and floral perfume ... It is the time to honour life in all its expression of abundance, profusion and sensuality. Life flows by voluptuously. Associated with heat, summer is a time of exuberance that favours expression.

☆ GUIDANCE ☆

Whatever season you are in, this card indicates a time of fulfilment, of shining and blooming. Connect to the sun, the emblem of summer, and awaken your sacred, joyful fire. Release your incredible creative energy. Forge ties with the medicine woman inside you, and affirm your talents with confidence. Celebrate your successes and openly shine! Love seems to smile upon you; give free rein to your sensuality and surrender to pleasure. Togetherness holds the place of honour – share and gather your loved ones around you. Life is one big party!

☆ AWAKEN THE MEDICINE ☆

In an echo of the summer season, open yourself up to the blossoming of who you are. To discover your unique perfume, take a ritual day off dedicated to the five senses, the gift of your incarnation. Touch: let the sun's rays, your lover's hand or a massage caress your body. Taste: enchant your taste buds with delicious dishes. Sight: contemplate a beautiful landscape or an exhibit. Sound: listen to the symphony of nature or sacred chants. Smell: re-enchant your nose with the perfume of flowers, aromatic spices or aphrodisiac ylang-ylang essential oil. By celebrating your five senses, you will shine the beauty of your sovereignty.

Give thanks. Make an offering to the sun – a poem or song or letting life voluptuously flow by.

MEDICINE
ACTION CARDS

To rehabilitate our original nature, we need to find
our medicine to heal the memories passed down since
the dawn of time, kindle the flame of pulsating life
and stand tall on the path of our rebirth. This active
practice proposes to heal the wounds of the past to
re-enchant the world with our divine presence, chants
and drums. It is the yang aspect of the wheel, a journey
of empowerment.

25. CREATIVE FIRE

REVEAL YOUR CREATIVE TALENT
FOR AN INSPIRED LIFE.

✖ MESSAGE ✖

Creativity reveals our soul path. We all have talents and resources just waiting to express themselves. A commanding creative impulse compels us to come out into the open, expose ourselves and breathe our specific artistic perfume into the world to embellish it, to kindle emotion and enchantment. This living river, which fertilises the most exuberant forms, flows naturally through women. To be creative is also to know the art of initiating your life by perceiving all the possibilities inside you. In native traditions, painting, dance and singing are principles of individual and collective regulation that keep a level of order in the community.

🏹 GUIDANCE 🏹

The time has come to warm your soul psyche before the fire of your inner wild woman's creative force. Go deep into your belly and heart to find that woman; she will plant seeds in your life. To rekindle your creative inspiration, ask yourself what brings you to life: dancing, poetry, singing, painting? You are invited to 'poetically and wildly inhabit your life', whispers analyst Clarissa Pinkola Estés. Whatever you are going through, you could receive transformation through the path of creation. Creativity brings profound liberation. Jump right in!

🏹 YOUR MEDICINE ACTION 🏹

Be wild, and cleanse the river! According to Clarissa Pinkola Estés: 'Creative flow is in us; it is rarely dried up but it can be polluted or contained.'

Creative practice. Light a candle, and invoke the spirit of creative fire. Breathe in deeply. Connect to the matrix of the second chakra, two fingers below your navel – your reservoir of creative impulse, your uterine cave, where the primordial feminine energies reside. Ask your question. Perform a sensory meditation with cinnamon bark essential oil. Let an image, sentence or thought come to you, and let the creative current course through you. Sing, dance, write and embrace life beating inside you. Stray off the beaten path, and lose sight of the end result. You are unique!

26. REBIRTH

× 26 ×
REBIRTH
AN OPPORTUNITY FOR DEEP TRANSFORMATION IS BEFORE YOU

AN OPPORTUNITY FOR DEEP TRANSFORMATION IS BEFORE YOU.

✗ MESSAGE ✗

Life is punctuated with passages. Birth is one of them, and along with death is probably the most important of all. Birth and death are two inverted movements. After sacred waiting comes the birthing process, a paroxysmal experience during which women discover an ancestral force, an unsuspected energy. Life can also bring an opportunity for rebirth, an initiation that will ask us, as a mother would, to open ourselves to the Great Mystery, trusting in the resources of our body and inner wisdom. It is the miracle of life!

✗ GUIDANCE ✗

A birth is in the works! This card indicates that it is time to give birth to yourself, saying 'Yes' to life. You are on the threshold of great transformation. You are probably carrying a foundational project for your evolution. What is this gift, talent or great love just waiting to hatch? At which stage are you in your sacred waiting to give birth to yourself? Do no try to hasten anything; everything is aligned! If you are expecting a child, you are both blessed and protected. Trust in yourself, and surround yourself with other women, midwives or doulas to accompany you on this passage.

✗ YOUR MEDICINE ACTION ✗

Ideally, you should embrace this powerful transformation while letting go, allowing the transformation to flow through you.

The practice of letting go. Invoke the medicine of the tortoise and its powerful grounding, for its unconditional support in bringing you where you are meant to be. Connect to your seventh chakra – the coronal chakra, celestial roots, your destiny. Perform a sensory meditation with frankincense with the intention of letting go. Embrace your fears, your limiting thoughts in the face of change, and release them. Trust in the mysterious pattern of life unfolding before you. Open yourself up to another dimension to let a better version of yourself come to life. The challenge you are invited to take up is to accept the loss of bearings that comes with great change.

If you are pregnant, you can offer your child a ritual love practice. Take some time to talk to your baby, croon to it, surround it with love and joy, and ask your body for support. What does your body need to provide your baby with the best nest it can possibly offer?

27. SISTERHOOD

INITIATE A NEW SISTERS' ADVENTURE.

 MESSAGE

In this period of great change, women are gathering in sisterhood with the intention of reconnecting to their true essence, reawakening their life force ... and changing the world. In times past, women gathered together and shared their knowledge, living and acting within women's circles.

When we listen to each woman's intimate stories, an ancestral truth emerges: we are all sisters, guardians of life. We are similar and yet all unique.

✕ GUIDANCE ✕

Remember, the hearts of women beat in unison; together, we are invincible. Yet the magic of sisterhood can only work once we heal the wounds of feminine rivalries. With whom are you in conflict: is it your mother, sister, friend, colleague? Each betrayal leaves a poison for which you must find the antidote. Life flows through us all, with great joys and hardships, births and losses, love and sickness ... like catalysts of our humanity. When you reconnect with trust you will recognise your allies.

✕ YOUR MEDICINE ACTION ✕

'We need allies; we need to be little wild mothers for each other, Baba Yagas,' says Clarissa Pinkola Estés.

Sisterhood practice. Join or initiate a women's circle, a protective cocoon dedicated to sisterhood. Women can come together in these cauldrons, these 'matrixes', as the crones call them. In these compassionate and confidential spaces, you can share your stories, secrets and wounds. Your intention is to gain a better understanding of feminine nature, reconnect with your gifts, cultivate a spirit of sisterhood … and heal the wounds of the past. Then you can forge profound ties of sisterhood to initiate a new adventure of women … who are now your sisters!

28. GRATITUDE

FEEL HOW LIFE SHOWERS YOU WITH BLESSINGS; GIVE THANKS!

✗ MESSAGE ✗

There is a magic ingredient to travelling the path of awakening the feminine – gratitude. The philosopher Epicurus sang its praises, and practised 'remembering beautiful things' as a spiritual exercise. We have forgotten that life is a permanent miracle, beginning with the miracle of our body. To honour one of the primordial laws of life – reciprocity – we can manifest our gratitude, thereby amplifying a positive outlook on our daily lives. When we apply this new perspective to our own lives we re-enchant them.

 GUIDANCE

This card indicates that today is the perfect day to choose gratitude: to savour your relationships, life and life's daily miracles. You may tend to always look for more, or better, or something different. The practice of gratitude rests on being able to embrace what presents itself while feeling joy that everything is already here. Try it! Your happiness is linked to what you experience in the moment, wherever you are. By celebrating life's generosity towards you, you reopen a virtuous circle in which you are showered with blessings.

YOUR MEDICINE ACTION

The teachings say it is good for the heart (in the sense of leading a happy life) to open and close the day by giving thanks.

Gratitude journal practice (for 21 days). When you wake up, take a short time – five minutes – to feel the miracle of life beating inside you and all around. At the end of each day, close your eyes and think of three things for which you feel grateful – words from someone you love, a success, the sun shining. It doesn't have to be spectacular. Write them in your notebook. Practise this as a ritual and ground positive values such as joy, optimism, generosity …

Collective sharing. When the time is right for you, suggest to your loved ones, or your partner, child or friends, that they share something positive for which they are grateful.

29. GROUNDING

BEING WELL GROUNDED PROVIDES A FEELING OF SECURITY.

⚔ MESSAGE ⚔

We are like majestic trees in a sacred forest. When we are well grounded we gracefully lift our branches towards the sky to receive information, and we take care of ourselves and our community. We preserve the memories of the past and witness our own destiny. Good grounding gives the feeling of being in your rightful place, and makes it possible to bring your projects and dreams for the future to life. Because we are manhandled by our lifestyles, without a powerful and fertile inner world we live off the ground! It can be difficult for us to set boundaries, bringing a feeling of insecurity.

↗ GUIDANCE ↗

You may be feeling harried by parasitic thoughts and mental chatter, which bring with them agitation and difficulty in making your aspirations a reality or making others respect your territory. It is time to relink with your ground connection, your grounding, to bring yourself back into precious presence of your own self and recapture your ability to carry out your projects. Your priority is to re-establish your sovereignty and be the queen of your kingdom!

↗ YOUR MEDICINE ACTION ↗

Inner world ritual. Stand tall. Anchor your feet into the ground. Feel their points of contact. Spread your toes. Imagine roots shooting deeply down into the earth. Breathe in, and let the energy rise up your legs and fill your pelvis and uterus, the seat of your power. Visualise an ancestral tree, the symbol of grounding. On the soles of your feet, dab a few drops of Atlas cedar essential oil to return your body to its life force and primordial instincts. For better grounding repeat the sound 'ouuu', sending this low-pitched tone, which carries great gentleness (a yin feminine quality), into your belly.

30. HEALING FAMILY LINES

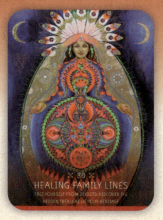

FREE YOURSELF FROM SECRETS;
DISCOVER THE HIDDEN TREASURE
OF YOUR HERITAGE.

 **MESSAGE**

Women, let us feel once again the beating pulse of our ancestors, our female line. Our mothers, grandmothers, great-grandmothers and their mothers before them have left us their legacy – memories and wounds passed down, as well as the knowledge of forgotten ancestral wisdom. There are signposts on our path to help us discover the earth from which we came, our principal wealth – our roots! Knowing them allows us to take our place on our family tree, free ourselves from secrets and raise ourselves straight and tall towards the sky!

✖ GUIDANCE ✖

It is time to rekindle the fire of your family line's memory to shed light on hidden areas and discover the gift of your heritage. Which ancestor stands beside you? You have an opportunity to reconnect with these feminine resources and the forgotten treasures they have bequeathed you. Perhaps you feel a transgenerational blockage. Release any imprint that does not belong to you. Remember, along with the trauma you carry the antidote. Discover the antidote so you can take your place on your family tree as a free woman and express your gifts.

✖ YOUR MEDICINE ACTION ✖

Healing family lines ritual. Gather photos of the women of your family line or images that symbolise them. Take up a percussion instrument such as a drum to bring on a light trance. Wrap a shawl around your shoulders to indicate you are ready for an intimate talk with the women of your line. Ask your questions. Which ancestor has a message for you? From which secret must you free yourself? What resource does that ancestor bequeath you? Let a healing song, the song of your matrix, your lineage, rise and ask the women for their support. When the time is right, place the shawl on the ground to give back to the earth what belongs to it.

Thank the earth and repeat the mantra: 'Today, I know where I come from. I honour my ancestors. I release what does not belong to me and I embrace the gift, the resource. I know where I'm going.' Trust in the process.

31. THE MALE PRINCIPLE

× 31 ×
THE MALE PRINCIPLE
A STEP TOWARDS RECONCILING WITH THE MASCULINE IS BEFORE YOU

A STEP TOWARDS RECONCILING WITH THE MASCULINE IS BEFORE YOU.

✗ MESSAGE ✗

At the heart of our quest is the union of our male and female polarities. Awakening the feminine rests on this path of reconciliation; we must overcome not only our internal conflicts but those revealed by our relationships.

Men are also on the move. Authenticity, responsibility and integrity are the keys of a new code of honour: to be a good knight and serve one's kingdom. Beyond existing models of the outdated patriarchy, the promise of a new dawn – where men rise with pride to be better and commit to building a safer world – is on the horizon.

⤜ GUIDANCE ⤜

This card indicates an opportunity of an encounter with the masculine; a man is presenting himself before you. Welcome him! Whether you are single or in a relationship, listen to the celestial music orchestrating your encounters. Each encounter is an opportunity to evolve. You are assured of being welcomed just as you are; this is a powerful vehicle of transformation for you both. Take the hand stretched out to you. He comes in peace, on the path that you can walk together. This card can also indicate an inner marriage of the male and female principles, which is a crucial step in the destiny of your love relationships.

⤜ YOUR MEDICINE ACTION ⤜

At what stage is your relationship with the masculine? You may have experienced setbacks or betrayals. It is time to forgive yourself, forgive the other and forgive the events that caused you pain.

Forgiveness ritual. Gather a notebook, pen and container. Draw a purification circle around you. Wrap a ritual shawl around your shoulders. Light a candle. Take up your drum, let a song rise up inside you and call the energy of forgiveness into your past relationships. What do you need to let go of? Which grievances? Write them down. Then, burn the piece of paper and feel your resentment being purified by fire. Let a feeling of compassion come to you, for yourself and for the other. Give thanks. Blow out the candle and close your circle. Then, let the cosmos orchestrate the great dance of love once more.

32. SPEAKING OUT

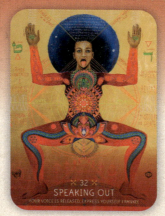

※ 32 ※
SPEAKING OUT
YOUR VOICE IS RELEASED; EXPRESS YOURSELF FRANKLY

YOUR VOICE IS RELEASED; EXPRESS YOURSELF FRANKLY.

✗ MESSAGE ✗

Behind the veils of the mystery of our being, a voice is
looking to make itself heard – our own unique voice!
Messenger of our intimacy expressing itself in the world,
our voice grows with us and evolves. From our first cry to

our final words, our voice says everything there is to know about us – our joys, troubles and desires. When we lose ourselves, our voice can sometimes hoarsen or disappear. The medicine of speaking out is our thread to move out of darkness or the shadows into light.

⤬ GUIDANCE ⤬

Freeing your voice will open the way of your destiny. Too long stifled or silenced, the voices of women are being released. It is no longer time for you to murmur or whisper, but to make your voice heard fully. Whatever the situation, express yourself authentically. Overcome your fears of being judged or rejected. What do you really have to say? Are you keeping a secret? Do you have anger inside you? This is the right time to break the silence and speak your truth. If you need help, turn towards sound, voice or song therapies for guidance.

⤬ YOUR MEDICINE ACTION ⤬

Make time to calm your voice so you can speak out clearly and without any aggressiveness.

Sacred vocal practice. In the Tibetan tradition, chanting the sound 'aaa' relaxes tension and anger. By opening the mouth and thus releasing the lower jaw, it thereby opens the door to cross the limits of the conscious. Sitting down, breathe in deeply. Then, breathing out, say 'aaa', opening your mouth wide. This sound invites your ordinary consciousness to relax and raises your vibratory rate. You are connected to the divine, to the luminous. You can now make space for considerate communication. If you find this difficult try breathing in ravintsara essential oil, which helps to regulate the throat chakra.

'Choose your words with care; they create the world around you.'

Navajo wisdom

33. THE ART OF RITUALS

PRACTISE RITUALS TO
RE-ENCHANT YOUR LIFE.

⚔ MESSAGE ⚔

With roots lost in the dawn of time, rites, ritual practices and festive ceremonies are ancestral activities related to habits and customs that structure our lives and communities. We need practices that reconnect us to the soul's symbolic language, to give meaning to our lives again and to feel the pulse and rhythm of important passages in life – births, weddings, deaths, seasonal cycles ... Let's celebrate and ritualise.

⤸ GUIDANCE ⤹

Remember the great feminine power of ritual arts. The time for sacred breaks has come; grant yourself these enchanted interruptions to lift the veil of mystery. Do you hear the call of magic? The soul works through magic! With all of life's vagaries, you have a vital need for ritual. What do you have to celebrate: a renewal, the end of a cycle, love coming back into your life? In the sacred space of contact with the divine – or consciousness – you can ask for what you truly want. Trust deeply that your prayer will be heard and answered. Your allies in the unseen realms are always by your side.

⤸ YOUR MEDICINE ACTION ⤹

On the night of a full or new moon, or at a solstice or equinox, or during time taken to return to yourself, bring ritual into your home sweet home.

Ritual creation practice. Create your own personal ceremony using a mix of sacredness and tradition. You will establish connection through a succession of simple actions acting as signals for your consciousness. Gather objects symbolising sacredness and relating to your request. Light a candle, wrap a shawl around your shoulders, connect to your unseen guide, dive into your depths and state your intention. Then the magic will awaken! Watch change unfold over the next few days.

'Rituals are a way of giving back to creation a little of the energy that we constantly receive.'

Wabun Wind,
Native American medicine woman

34. THE MOON

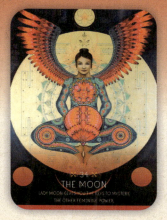

LADY MOON GIVES YOU THE KEYS TO MYSTERY, THE OTHER FEMININE POWER.

⚔ MESSAGE ⚔

I expand; I wax and wane; I influence the tides, women's cycles and births. I am the moon goddess Selene, and I was worshipped long ago. Can you feel how close we are?

An ancestral story plays itself out between women and the moon. In ancient traditions, priestesses worshipped Selene or Hecate in connection with the creative and fertile power of Lady Moon. Our feminine cycle synchronising with the cycle of the moon and tides reminds us of our deeply mysterious connection. Births are governed by the moon. Seemingly softer moonlight lights the worlds of shadow, instinct and the unconscious. The moon is the seat of women's fertile power. In the night, its gentle and benevolent power opens the door to dreams, another reality.

⚔ GUIDANCE ⚔

The moon is a powerful ally for your psyche and fertile power; the moon reminds you of its presence by your side. Perhaps you have forgotten your lunar, poetic and sorceress self. Like the moon, you fluctuate in the ebb and flow of your inner life, curious of the secrets hidden in the shadows and deeps ... You may feel an irrational desire for another reality of fairyland and spells. Call upon the moon for all your projects. The new moon, a protective mother, acts like a charm to bring you abundance and respond favourably to your wishes. The full moon takes you into the depths of your true nature.

⤢ YOUR MEDICINE ACTION ⤢

Plan for moon rituals.

New moon ritual. Dedicated to Hecate, this is a time for renewal and wishes. Fill a bowl with water and drop a moonstone in it. Invoke the goddess, asking her to protect you and stating your wish from the heart, trusting in her generosity. Let a prayer, song or dance rise up inside you. Put your bowl outside. Early the next morning, drink the water charged by the moon and let its energy fill your heart.

Full moon ritual. Dedicated to Selene, this is a time for celebration. Take a moonstone in your hands. Invoke the goddess. Take a moonlight bath, visualising a luminous white circle around you … Ask the goddess to reveal your lunar talent as a sacred woman by sending you a dream. Let a prayer, song or dance rise up inside you. When you wake up, write down your dream in your notebook.

35. EMPOWERMENT

ASSERT YOURSELF, AND SHINE YOUR POWER. NOW!

✗ MESSAGE ✗

A woman's true value is a jewel waiting to shine. Even today, women's self-confidence remains unconquered territory. This is due to the patriarchal system, in which our relationship to men (as protectors, predators or work supervisors) has deeply inscribed in us feeling dependent on them financially, physically and socially. Although this is beginning to change, that ancestral imprint is still present. A new step is now presenting itself to us – the opportunity to contact our feminine power and take back our leadership.

✘ GUIDANCE ✘

Your new goal is empowerment. Cultivate the profound conviction that, as a woman, you represent a factor of positive change to build a more loving, respectful and environmentally protective world. What challenge must you take up to take your place and show your ambition? What great project do you dream of? It is time to free yourself from old models and participate fully in the world. Your new aces are following your intuition, valuing your emotions and relying on authenticity and collective intelligence. Assert yourself, and let your power shine. Now!

✘ YOUR MEDICINE ACTION ✘

Success journal practice. To strengthen your gifts and gain in self-confidence, begin by identifying them. Learn to celebrate your victories, large and small! Do not apologise for your successes. Learn to congratulate yourself. If a compliment comes your way, welcome it and feel it. Feel your energy beaming with gratitude. Practising empowerment highlights the importance of pointing to what makes you shine. Now, decide to take back your personal power! By positively signposting the progress you've already made, you will shine light on your strong points – what makes you unique – and increase your self-esteem.

36. PURIFICATION

×36×
PURIFICATION
RAISE YOUR VIBRATIONS BY CARING FOR YOUR ENERGY

RAISE YOUR VIBRATIONS BY CARING FOR YOUR ENERGY.

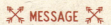 **MESSAGE**

We are vibratory beings! At the heart of our evolution is
the energy dimension of our being. Becoming aware of this
potential can increase our subtle feelings and, at the same
time, recharge our energy. This opens us to new fields of

understanding life's true nature. We are energy, and we can be channels of divine and terrestrial energy to create fulfilling lives for ourselves in accord with universal laws – as long as we purify our energies, or auras.

✗ GUIDANCE ✗

This card is an invitation to take care of your energy. Remember, we are like sponges: we soak up everything, positive or negative. Check where you are at in terms of energy. Depending on who you were with, you may already have felt yourself being rejuvenated or exhausted. Places also have an impact on your energy. This is particularly so for sensitive people when they find themselves in a crowd, store or subway ... It is vital for you learn to protect yourself, and to rest and recuperate regularly to pulsate with energy – that is your true nature.

✗ YOUR MEDICINE ACTION ✗

Protection bubble practice. Make a consciously aware diagnosis of your energy. How do you feel: are you full of joy and exuberance, or flat and listless? What you feel may be subtle, but it can be discerned like heaviness, fatigue or sadness.

In this practice, the process involves releasing what weighs on you and expressing things in a positive way.

Sitting with your legs crossed, visualise being showered with golden white light that is purifying your energy. Say: 'I release ...' Let this energy cleanse your three energy centres – your third eye (or your consciousness), heart and uterus. Draw a circle around the earth–sky axis, from right to left and then from left to right, while visualising a bubble of light in which the words 'energy', 'positive', 'love' and 'beauty' glitter. Give thanks.

ACKNOWLEDGEMENTS

Oracle cards are a particular passion of mine. They are such a feminine divination support, and a magical gateway to the unseen – to mystery, archetypes, our guides and all our allies on different planes. As an author, embarking on this adventure was a revelation, blessing and deeply transformative journey.

I have infinite gratitude to my teachers, thanks to whom I have fertilised the seeds of my dream and gained confidence in my talent. Thank you to Carol Anpo Wi and the loyal Keepers of the 13 Moons; to Agnès Addey, who opened my mind to the therapeutic genius of plants; to Else Oreve and her drum circles; to Marie Motais, Ya'Acov and Susannah Darling Khan, for the awakening of my shamanic body through dance; to Marianne Grasselli Meier, wonderful earth guardian; and to analyst and storyteller Clarissa Pinkola Estés, my first source of inspiration.

Thank you to my Mother Bear, my Snowy Owl, and my Pépita Pink Flamingo, my fabulous shamanic allies, who never let me down by a feather or hair on my journey.

Thank you to my women's line – Louise, my wonderful mother; Suzanne and Marie-Jeanne, my grandmothers; and the women whose names I do not yet know – and to Pachamama, the mother of all women.

Infinite gratitude to Caroline Manière and her divine medicine women, the heroines of this project; they probably weaved this dream long before we did. Thanks to my loyal ally and friend Cathy Selena of Le Courrier du Livre and to Séverine Joaquim, our graphic design fairy.

Thank you to all my women's rituals sisters, with whom I share the adventure of awakening the feminine ...

Catherine Maillard

I pay homage to the medicine women, who came to me to shine their universal message of love, kindness, healing and teachings.

All my thanks to Marco, my precious partner, for his support and unwavering trust during all the years he allowed me to spread my wings and embrace these medicine women.

And thank you to Catherine, for having the talent, experience and knowledge to bring the medicine women together in a circle and create this superb oracle.

Caroline Manière

BIBLIOGRAPHY

A selection of works and their authors are powerful allies on my journey of deepening my knowledge and awakening the feminine. Here I would like to thank these women, these most inspiring authors and guides on our path.

Bear, Sun, Wind, Wabun and Mulligan, Crysalis, *Dancing with the Wheel: The Medicine Wheel Workbook,* Simon & Schuster, 1991.

Diamant, Anita, *The Red Tent*, St Martin's Press, 1997.

Estés, Clarissa Pinkola, *Women Who Run with the Wolves: Myths and Stories of the Wild Woman Archetype*, Ballantine Books, 1996.

Harding, M. Esther, *Woman's Mysteries: Ancient and Modern*, Shambhala, 2001.

Ingerman, Sandra and Roberts, Llyn, *Speaking with Nature: Awakening to the Deep Wisdom of the Earth*, Bear & Company, 2015.

Miller, Madeleine, *Circe*, Little, Brown and Company, 2018.

Sams, Jamie, *The 13 Original Clan Mothers: Your Sacred Path to Discovering the Gifts, Talents, and Abilities of the Feminine Through the Ancient Teachings of the Sisterhood*, Harper Collins, 1994.

Schaefer, Carol, *Grandmothers Counsel the World: Women Elders Offer Their Vision for Our Planet*, Trumpeter, 2006.

(Available in French)

Colonna, Marie-Laure, *Réenchanter l'Occident*, Éditions Entrelacs, 2019.

Meier, Marianne Grasselli, *Le Réveil des gardiennes de la terre*, Le Courrier du Livre, 2018.

Quentin, Florence, *Isis l'Éternelle. Biographie d'un mythe feminine*, Éditions Albin Michel, 2012.

ABOUT THE AUTHOR

Catherine Maillard is a journalist, editor, author and creator of the 'Awakening the Feminine' and 'Women's Rituals' collections. She is a facilitator of women's circles with 20 years of experience in shamanic practices (Emaho, Patricia Buffalo White, Else Oreve, Marie Motais, Ya'Acov and Suzannah Darling Khan), dance therapy, the teachings of the Keepers of the 13 Moons (Carol Anpo Wi), and training in sensitive aromatherapy, encountering the therapeutic genius of plants (Agnès Addey). She is also trained in applied relaxology (the Vittoz approach) and rebirth (Association Oser).

Catherine's commitment to ecofeminism stems from a deep desire to weave new ties between women and nature, between ecology and feminism – an alliance that could well mark the beginning of major change.

www.catherine-maillard.com
facebook.com/catherine.maillard.902
www.instagram.com/catherine.maillard.rituels

PUBLISHED BOOKS (IN FRENCH)

Rituels de femmes pour s'éveiller au féminin sauvage, co-authored with Isabelle Gueudré, Éd. Le Courrier du Livre, 2016.

J'ai mal à mes ancêtres. La psychogénéalogie aujourd'hui, co-authored with Patrice Van Eersel, Éd. Albin Michel, 2012.

Je danse donc j'existe. Le grand boum de la danse-thérapie, Éd. Albin Michel, 2015.

ABOUT THE ARTIST

Caroline Manière is an artist whose role is to share a message through her painting. She paints with the intention that each work carries a frequency of healing and awakening.

With each brush stroke she follows her intuition, letting the colours and symbols come to her; she is a tool at the service of what her essence wants to communicate, for you and as many people as possible. She is the link between two worlds who listens to her heart and lets herself be guided.

Caroline paints on sheets of copper or gold, because she loves the light that comes to envelop these women and brings them respect, sacredness and majesty.

Since 2015 these medicine women, animals, totems and Caroline's little clay dolls, the Medicine Mamas, have shared universal messages of love, knowledge, wisdom, guidance and support.

www.carolinemaniere.com
facebook.com/caroline.maniere
facebook.com/carolinemanierefemmesmedecine
www.instagram.com/carolinemaniere